STEM-Infusing the Elementary Classroom

To Clark—my favorite little engineer

STEM-Infusing the Elementary Classroom

Miranda Talley Reagan

Foreword by Cary Sneider

CORWIN
A SAGE Publishing Company

FOR INFORMATION:

Corwin

A SAGE Company

2455 Teller Road

Thousand Oaks, California 91320

(800) 233-9936

www.corwin.com

SAGE Publications Ltd.

1 Oliver's Yard

55 City Road

London EC1Y 1SP

United Kingdom

SAGE Publications India Pvt. Ltd.

B 1/I 1 Mohan Cooperative Industrial Area

Mathura Road, New Delhi 110 044

India

SAGE Publications Asia-Pacific Pte. Ltd.

3 Church Street

#10-04 Samsung Hub

Singapore 049483

Acquisitions Editor: Erin Null

Editorial Development Manager: Julie Nemer

Senior Associate Editor: Desirée A. Bartlett

Editorial Assistants: Andrew Olson and
                                        Nicole Shade

Production Editor: Melanie Birdsall

Copy Editor: Grace Kluck

Typesetter: Hurix Systems Pvt. Ltd.

Proofreader: Lawrence W. Baker

Indexer: Amy Murphy

Cover Designer: Janet Kiesel

Marketing Manager: Margaret O'Connor

Chapter-opening photos by Miranda Talley Reagan.

Printed in the United States of America

Library of Congress Cataloging-in-Publication Data

Names: Reagan, Miranda Talley, author.

Title: STEM-infusing the elementary classroom / Miranda Talley Reagan.

Description: Thousand Oaks, California : Corwin, A SAGE Company, 2016. | Includes bibliographical references and index.

Identifiers: LCCN 2015040111 | ISBN 9781483392363 (pbk. : alk. paper)

Subjects: LCSH: Education, Elementary—Activity programs. | Science—Study and teaching (Elementary) | Mathematics—Study and teaching (Elementary) | Interdisciplinary approach in education.

Classification: LCC LB1592 .R43 2016 | DDC 372.3—dc23 LC record available at http://lccn.loc.gov/2015040111

This book is printed on acid-free paper.

SUSTAINABLE FORESTRY INITIATIVE

Certified Chain of Custody

Promoting Sustainable Forestry

www.sfiprogram.org

SFI-01268

SFI label applies to text stock

16 17 18 19 20 10 9 8 7 6 5 4 3 2 1

Contents

Foreword

A few years ago, I had the good fortune to serve on the writing team for the Next Generation Science Standards. More than 50 percent of our team members were active teachers, and most of the rest of us had been teachers for at least part of our career. Our goal, which I think we largely achieved, was to project a new vision for science teaching. To realize this vision, the core ideas that we used to think of as our most important learning goals—what we used to call the *content*—become deeply entwined with technology, engineering, and mathematics. The vision, in other words, was that "science" teaching be replaced with integrated "STEM" teaching.

Since my lifetime of experiences have focused almost entirely on the middle and high school levels, I was not sure how the vision of integrated STEM would play out at the elementary level. I was skeptical because few elementary teachers have college degrees in STEM fields, and research shows that very little time is devoted to science teaching at the elementary level. However, my colleagues on the writing team who were elementary teachers moved forward with confidence and stories of personal experiences that convinced me it was possible. In fact, they said that elementary teachers had the advantage that they taught all subjects, so it should be easier for them to teach integrated STEM and even use some time formerly devoted entirely to social studies and English to teach integrated STEM units.

I was still somewhat skeptical when I received an invitation to write a foreword to this book. But after reading a few chapters my skepticism melted away. What we have in this short volume is both an existence proof that integrated STEM can be taught at the earliest elementary grade levels and a set of clear and compelling guidelines for how to make it happen. The author has also provided us with a very enjoyable reading experience, complete with humorous vignettes and short but richly textured examples.

The book is very well organized, starting with a few chapters that establish what the author means by STEM-infusion and a well thought out rationale for why STEM-infusion is important for children's growth and development. The theory, which supports the author's rationale, is based on recent scientific research and simply put. Later chapters provide general methods for developing STEM-infused lessons, and the last chapter offers ideas for engaging other teachers, parents, and administrators. Individual chapters are also well organized, ending with a few questions to spark discussion with colleagues and suggestions for how to begin implementing activities suggested in the chapter.

One of the ideas that resonated especially strongly with my own experience as a science educator is the pendulum metaphor for periodic swings in emphasis between broad process skills versus achievement of specific standards. The author makes a plea for balance and reinforces this commitment throughout the book by illustrating how lessons that enable children to develop such broad process skills as critical thinking, communication, and collaboration can also help them achieve specific measurable capabilities in STEM subject areas. Consequently, we often run across the words "creativity" and "rigor" when reading about a single lesson.

The author occasionally goes beyond the core subject matter of STEM-infusion and touches on broader educational issues, such as assessment, social-emotional skills, and engaging parents. She offers her own viewpoint and wise counsel on controversial issues. For example, after a short discussion of her role as coordinator of mandated state testing in her school, she concludes,

> But for all the controversy that surrounds standardized testing, there is one thing we teachers need not lose sight of: assessing our students and meeting their individual needs based on those assessments is about a moral imperative, not a state mandate. In other words, we owe it to our kids to do a good job of keeping check on where they are, to what extent they are meeting their goals, and what skill gaps are forming. And then we must provide what they need to extend those skills, fill in gaps, and set new goals.

What I enjoyed most about the book were the examples in which the author explained how she learned from her students. One was a fourth grader who noticed that all of the subjects she was teaching had to do with cyclic patterns, helping her focus on the value of organizing the curriculum by crosscutting concepts. While that was something she may have done subconsciously, her student helped her recognize the value of planning a sequence of lessons to make crosscutting concepts visible. Later in the book she tells the reader that her elementary students help her determine what criteria to include in the rubrics that she uses to assess their work.

I trust you will enjoy the book as much as I did and that you'll find in it not just nuggets of information but a mother lode of inspiration combined with sound practical ideas for infusing STEM into your school's curriculum.

—Cary Sneider
Associate Research Professor, Portland State University

Preface

My son was born a builder. From the time he developed the least amount of motor control, he built towers, castles, and bridges out of everything from blocks to the little plastic creamer cups for the coffee at IHOP. He learns by exploring. He grows by creating, testing, and improving his design. He is a natural engineer.

If you have children, this may sound familiar. This approach to learning is nearly universal among babies and toddlers. Babies put everything in their mouths because they are experimenting and exploring. They learn from the effects of every move they make. They build up a mental library of experiences and information through every action. And if you are an elementary teacher, you also know that this is not the exclusive practice of babies. Children continue to learn through trial and error (for as long as we let them).

This is what STEM-infusion is all about. It's about capitalizing on a child's natural curiosity, the need to understand, the desire to try something and see what the outcome will be. As seems appropriate, in our school, STEM-infusion is a model of teaching that was developed by accident. Just like we ask our students to do in a STEM-infused classroom, my colleagues and I have developed, tweaked, and improved this method of teaching through trial and error. In order to understand exactly what this method is, it's important to hear the backstory of how we came to use it in our school.

OUR ROAD TO STEM-INFUSION

I live in a fairly small city school district. We have one high school, one junior high, two intermediate schools, and three elementary schools. Our district consistently ranks among the top performing districts in the state of Tennessee. But several years ago, as part of our strategic plan, we decided to enhance our math and science programs in order to graduate students who were better prepared for 21st century colleges and the workforce. In an effort to do so, the district decided to introduce STEM classes at the intermediate, middle, and high school levels and purchase

Project Lead the Way curriculum for those programs. However, after considering the justification for STEM education (found in Chapter 2 of this book), our administrators decided that STEM should be taught at all grade levels, starting in kindergarten.

At the time I was a fourth-grade math and science teacher in one of our elementary schools and when the position was posted for elementary STEM, I decided to apply. Although I had only recently heard of STEM, the concept of integrating subjects through creative design resonated with me. To me, it made sense to teach that way. After I was hired to teach my kindergarten through third grade STEM class, I was given the charge of researching what STEM would look like at the elementary level and the freedom to design the course according to that research. Little did I know what a challenge that would be. At the time, there was very little content to be found about STEM in elementary school. That summer, however, I attended the National Science Teachers Association (NSTA) STEM forum, which really helped me envision how an elementary STEM class might look.

When our first year of STEM began, the class was built around the engineering design process (ask, imagine, plan, create, and improve). I primarily attempted to connect the engineering projects to the science standards for each grade level. For example, when the students learned about habitats, each group designed a habitat for a hermit crab (see Figure P.1). The students researched what food, water source, shelter, etc. a hermit crab would live in and built a habitat in a plastic box. We connected those habitats using plastic tubes and placed four hermit crabs in the center box. Each day, the students would graph where the hermit crabs were living and make adjustments to their habitat in an attempt to better attract the crabs. Although this plan to connect science and the engineering design process served us well that first year, it was only the first step in our journey. Deep connections to math and technology were lacking that year as the program was being developed.

The following summer, however, my whole philosophy of STEM changed. I attended the Tennessee STEM Teachers Academy, which was organized by the Tennessee STEM Network and the Oak Ridge Associated Universities. That summer, my colleague, Dee Dulin, and I heard Dr. Tony Donen, principal of STEM School Chattanooga, talk about his high school that totally integrated their entire curriculum through design projects. He described how all of their departments (language, math, science, social studies, arts, physical education, humanities, etc.) worked together to come up with semester-long projects in which the students would use all of the skills and coursework to build a solution to an engineering challenge. After hearing about their success, we felt that we had short-changed STEM's potential by simply teaching it one hour a week in isolation from the rest of the curriculum. Instead, we began to build the idea of STEM-infusing elementary classrooms. Dee, who is a first-grade teacher, and I prepared model lessons to show our faculty. Instead of long-term projects, we felt that a week-long project integrating the content covered that week would be ideal. Dee demonstrated

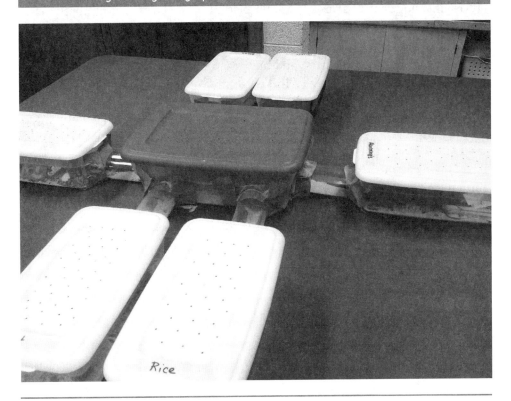

Figure P.1 Third graders designed hermit crab habitats, tracked the movement of live hermit crabs, and improved their habitats using the engineering design process.

SOURCE: **Photo by Linda Talley.**

what we would eventually come to call the thematic approach to STEM-infusion (Chapter 6) with a first-grade lesson, and I showed the standards alignment approach (Chapter 5) with a third-grade lesson.

Buy-in for this new concept began with a small minority—just a couple of teachers on each team. However, the STEM-infusion movement began to take root as those energetic pioneers shared their ideas and resources with their teams. By the third year of STEM in our school, over half of our faculty was using STEM-infusion regularly, while many others were beginning to understand the relevance of this teaching model in preparing kids to live in the 21st century.

At the same time, our district began a one-to-one device initiative, and we got iPads in the elementary schools. As our district developed a philosophy of utilizing devices to supplement effective teaching strategies and as a platform to create, research, and innovate, it became clear that our vision for STEM-infusion and the district's vision for technology integration would be mutually beneficial. In fact, many of our teachers felt like they were ahead of the game when it came to technology integration because with the new way they were teaching, the need for technology was there. It was not just about trying to figure out how to fit technology in, it was about using technology to enhance the project-based learning and STEM-infusion that was already taking place. During that exciting first year of technology (which was our third year of STEM), I served as our school's Instructional Coach for STEM and Technology Integration. My job was essentially to help teachers plan, implement, and improve STEM and technology-integrated activities. By the end of that year, 100 percent of our teachers had used STEM-infusion to some extent, over half using it daily. Most of the lessons you will read about in this book are lessons that I co-planned or co-taught with other kindergarten through third-grade teachers.

As this book is in final drafts, I am beginning a new adventure in my STEM journey. This year, I will be a third-grade teacher. I will get to experience my own STEM-infused classroom full-time. I cannot express how excited I am about this or how fully I believe in STEM's potential to engage students, facilitate positive collaboration, deepen understanding of academic concepts, and foster the ability to innovate.

STEM-INFUSION

If you have read anything on elementary STEM before, chances are this book will be a bit different. Instead of approaching STEM as a subject or a type of activity, we will explore STEM-infusion as a teaching model to integrate all content areas in a way that provides rich meaningful experiences for students.

OVERVIEW OF THE BOOK

Chapters 1 and 2 will introduce the concept and provide a rationale for STEM-infusion. Next (Chapter 3), we will look at STEM-infusion as a solution to the need for lessons with high rigor and high relevance. After that, in Chapters 4 to 6, I will explain and model various approaches to STEM-infusion in an elementary classroom. The remainder (Chapters 7 to 10) will address the other important issues related to STEM-infusion, such as assessment, teaching grit, student and teacher collaboration, and leading educational change.

FEATURES AND BENEFITS

The book also includes the following additional resources to help you get started on your journey toward STEM-infusion.

- **Classroom Vignettes.** Each chapter will provide information from the perspective of someone who has experienced STEM-integration first-hand, in a way that is easy to read and immediately applicable to your practice as a classroom teacher, instructional coach, or administrator.

- **Glossary.** Each time you come to a bolded word while reading, you can look in the glossary for a more detailed definition.

- **Discussion Starters.** These discussion questions will help you and your teammates understand and apply the information in each chapter.

- **Your Next Step.** These teacher challenges encourage you to move forward in your STEM-infusion journey after each chapter.

- **Photographs.** Photographs in this book will help you envision the activities being described in each chapter.

- **Sample Lesson Plans.** The sample lesson plans explain the lessons described in the chapters in more detail and are found in the Resources section.

- **Lesson Plan Templates.** These resources can be used in planning your own STEM-infused lessons and are found in the Resources section.

- **Additional STEM Challenge Ideas.** These resources will get you started brainstorming your own STEM-infusion ideas and are found in the Resources section.

TESTIMONIALS

STEM-infusion has completely transformed the way I teach and the way I learn. And I am most definitely not the only one. Here are a few examples of perspectives on STEM-infusion:

It has been exciting to see the results of our STEM-infusion efforts unfold in our elementary classrooms. Teachers have collaborated across schools and grade levels to provide students with stimulating project-based experiences. Seeing students use the engineering design process to solve problems and draw conclusions from their work is evidence of a true shift in practice for us.

—Dr. Mike Winstead, Director of Schools, Maryville City Schools (Maryville, TN)

STEM-infused instruction has totally changed the dynamics of the instruction at our school. Our teachers are facilitators and students have ownership in their learning. Through this rigorous instruction our students develop the valuable life skills of productive struggle, problem solving, and collaboration.

—Mr. Scott Blevins, Principal, Sam Houston Elementary School (Maryville, TN)

STEM-infusion in my first-grade classroom has allowed students from all ability levels to make more connections within our curriculum, overcome challenges by using multiple problem-solving strategies, and develop relationships with peers based on considerate listening and respectful talk. Plus, most of my students would say it's their favorite part of our classroom!

—Mrs. Dee Dulin, First-Grade Teacher, Sam Houston Elementary School (Maryville, TN)

WHAT YOU WILL GET OUT OF THIS BOOK

If you are a K–5 teacher, principal, instructional coach, or curriculum coordinator, this book is for you! It will help you do the following:

- Understand a need for STEM-infusion and help you communicate that need to your colleagues.

- Implement STEM-infusion and apply it your to your existing curriculum.

- Integrate content areas in a way that brings both rigor and relevance to your instruction.

- Foster 21st century skills of communication, collaboration, critical thinking, and creativity in both your students and faculty.

I cannot wait to share what I have learned in my classroom and the classrooms of my colleagues in the past few years. Let's get started!

Acknowledgments

The past five years, I have been blessed with what Ephesians 3:20 calls "exceedingly and abundantly more than I could ever imagine." I count my opportunities and experiences with STEM among the top of that list of blessings and thank the Lord for these experiences.

Thanks so much to my wonderful husband! His love and support have been the backdrop of every one of the experiences described in this book. He makes me laugh hysterically but also models a quiet humility. And his first grade students are so lucky to have such an amazing teacher.

To my son, Clark, I love you! You are the reason I do what I do. You are the reason I want to be a part of this change in the way we do school. You are the reason I want to help mold the future. I am so incredibly blessed to have a little buddy who loves creative design as much as I do. Thank you for STEM-infusing our home with me!

I want to thank my parents who took me on adventures, encouraged me to take risks, modeled the essential lesson that success starts with relationships, celebrated all four of us kids as different as we all were, and made us believe we could do anything. (It is only now that I am a mom that I am truly learning to appreciate how hard all that is.) They taught me that life is all about the journey. And that has been my inspiration throughout my career so far.

Thank you to my friends and colleagues at Sam Houston Elementary who have discovered STEM-infusion along with me. I especially want to thank Dee and Kyle, who have walked with me in each step of this process—defining STEM-infusion, writing lessons, sharing with other teachers, brainstorming during the writing process, editing and revising my writing, and generally encouraging me. I also want to thank Suzanne and Erica who have been much more than teaching assistants. They have been encouragers, collaborators, and friends.

I also want to express my appreciation for the administration both at my school and at our district. They have prioritized STEM, technology, and 21st century skills for our students through their support, resources, autonomy, and encouragement for teachers. Scott, Glenn, Ashley, Mike, Rick, Amy, Jan, and Andrew—thank you!

Thank you to all the students who have fallen in love with STEM-infusion along with me! We have had such an adventure together. Murphy, Bailey, Finn, Anna Claire, Nick, Wyatt, Sara, Mia, Landen, Noah, Grant, Grant, Abby, Brooklyn, Madi, Saniyah, Kiyana, Caroline, Anna, and Sean—you inspire me every day! Special thanks to the kiddos (and their parents) who allowed me to include their pictures in this book. And a huge thank you to my aunt, Linda, who contributed her talent for photography in taking these pictures.

Thanks to my Faith Promise family and small group. I cannot imagine what the past few years would have been like without them. Although most have not necessarily been a part of the experiences in this book (and probably will never see this page), they have helped to shape me into the person I am. Therefore, they have had an enormous impact on the "me" that readers will perceive on these pages.

I also want to thank those who have played a part in my education in Maryville City Schools, Maryville College, and Lincoln Memorial University. Through their example, they taught me how to actively love my students, set a fire in me for lifelong learning, and inspired my passion for continuous improvement.

And to my new friends at Corwin—thank you for this opportunity to share what I love with other people. Ariel, Desirée, Andrew, Grace, Melanie, and everyone else at Corwin who touches this book, thank you for taking a chance on me and walking me through the process.

PUBLISHER'S ACKNOWLEDGMENTS

Corwin gratefully acknowledges the contributions of the following reviewers:

Marsha Basanda
Fifth-Grade Teacher
Monarch Elementary
Simpsonville, SC

Stacey Ferguson
K–6 Teacher
Bay-Waveland Schools
Bay St. Louis, MS

Marti Hooten
Teacher
Leaphart Elementary School
Columbia, SC

Alexis Ludewig
Retired Elementary Teacher
University of Wisconsin
    Oshkosh
Oshkosh, WI

Christine Ruder
Third-Grade Teacher
Truman Elementary School
Rolla, MO

Nicholas Rudman
Head Teacher
Maylandsea Community
    Primary School
Chelmsford, UK

Joyce Sager
Inclusion Math Teacher
Gadsden City High School
Gadsden, AL

Susan Schipper
Elementary Teacher
Charles Street School
Palmyra, NJ

Craig Yen
Fifth-Grade Teacher
Mt. Diablo Unified School District
Concord, CA

About the Author

 **Miranda Talley Reagan** began her career as a fourth-grade teacher with an appreciation for hands-on learning and helping students make connections across content areas. When her school system began a K–12 STEM initiative, she was hired to develop and implement an elementary STEM curriculum for a K–3 STEM lab. During her two years in the STEM lab, Miranda logged her elementary STEM lab experiences on a blog on her school website, which has become a popular resource for elementary STEM teachers nationwide and even internationally.

After the success of the STEM lab, Miranda accepted a year-long position as Instructional Coach for STEM and Technology Integration. During this time, she led an initiative in her own school while also working with other schools interested in STEM-integration.

Miranda has now transitioned back into a third-grade classroom in order to practice STEM-infusion full time. She continues to be a teacher leader within her school as well as providing professional development for other districts.

Miranda has a bachelor's degree in child development and learning, a master's in curriculum and instruction, and an educational specialist degree in educational leadership.

CHAPTER 1

STEM-Infusing All Content Areas

A WAY OF TEACHING

In its most basic definition, **STEM-infusion** means using the concepts that are part of STEM (such as the **engineering design process**, creativity, collaboration, problem solving, and technology integration) to teach or practice all subjects in the elementary classroom. The teacher sets up a **design challenge** in which the students learn about and integrate ideas from various subjects in order to create a solution to the problem. For example, in a fourth-grade classroom, the teacher may plan to cover the following subjects during a week:

- **English/Language Arts.** Cause and effect
- **Math.** Triangles
- **Social Studies.** Branches of government, checks and balances
- **Science.** Environmental impacts

All of these topics can be tied together by presenting students with an engineering challenge that applies to current events. In this challenge, the students are answering the following **essential question**: Should the Keystone Pipeline be allowed? (See Resource A.) (At the time this book was written, President Obama had vetoed the bill. However, this topic is an excellent opportunity to understand our government and allow students to compile evidence to defend their ideas.)

The lesson begins with students doing background research to understand the branches of government, the process of a bill becoming a law, and the system of checks and balances. I, as the teacher, provide videos, articles, and discussion questions through Blackboard, our learning management system. However, if you do not have a similar system, Padlet is a free website that allows you to build a webpage of various digital resources very easily.

After the students have a basic understanding of our government, I present them with an article about the Keystone bill. The article is balanced in its political views and describes the supporter's viewpoints on increasing jobs and financial benefits and the opposition's stands on environmental impacts. It also includes a map of the proposed Keystone pipeline and the existing one. Since the two form a triangle, the students can use their geometry skills to determine the difference in distance oil would travel in the two pipelines. I then encourage the students to look at a historical perspective to create a list of pros and cons for the pipeline. Fortunately, the Scott Foresman fourth-grade reading basal includes a leveled reader on the Alaskan Pipeline. The students use this reader to develop a pros and cons graphic. So far, this sounds like a social studies lesson with some reading and science integrated, right? But this is where the design challenge comes in!

Now, the students have to "put themselves on a line." The students have a pipeline labeled 1 to 10: 1 being completely for the pipeline and 10 being completely against it. They decide where they would rank their opinions at that point. Then I proceed to partner them up with someone who believes very differently on the issue. The design challenge is to build a pipeline that allows 200 ml of water to run a distance of 1 meter from one cup to another (see Figure 1.1). The students may use craft sticks, cardboard tubes, foam cups, straws, paper, tape, etc. to build their pipeline. This is an interesting challenge because the students first have to figure out that ALL of the water has to run downhill in order for the pipeline to work. It sounds obvious but so many students poke a hole in the side of the first cup instead of the bottom so some water is trapped from the get-go. Also, the students really struggle to keep their pipeline from leaking.

The really interesting and beneficial part of this challenge, however, is the conversation between the two students who have very different concerns for their pipeline. The "big oil" student is worried about profit loss if the pipeline leaks, while the "environmentalist" worries about the effects of an oil spill. The students get so involved in the project they treat it as if it were real. And suddenly all of these big ideas—cause and effect, government, geometry, environment—have a real world context.

> Figure 1.1 Students designed and improved a pipeline as they learned about environmental issues and government in third-grade social studies.

SOURCE: Photo by Linda Talley.

MISCONCEPTIONS ABOUT STEM-INFUSION

EC⁴S³TREAM is an acronym that stands for Engineering, Creativity, Collaboration, Communication, Critical thinking, Science, Social Studies, Technology, Reading, English, Arts, and Mathematics.... Okay, I cannot even say that sentence out loud with a straight face. And that, right there, is the reason this book is titled *STEM-Infusing the Elementary Classroom.*

More times than I can count, when I have explained the concept of STEM-infusion to someone, I have heard responses such as the following:

- "Oh, you're integrating arts into STEM.... You should really call that STEAM."
- "Since you're using STEM to teach reading and arts, that should be labeled STREAM."
- "Isn't what you're really describing more like project-based learning than STEM? I don't think people in the hard sciences would consider that 'pure STEM.'"
- "Oh, yeah.... That's just thematic teaching. That was a fad back when I started teaching before high stakes testing came along. I think it's funny that the pendulum is starting to swing back toward a thematic approach to teaching again."

If you too had one of these thoughts when you first picked up this book, I understand the confusion completely. There are so many acronyms that have become spin-offs of STEM, it can be confusing to figure out exactly what we're talking about here. To clarify, I will respond to each of the statements above.

- Creativity is embedded in the engineering design process. Therefore, I do not feel it is essential to include the word "art" in my acronym since I believe art is implied as part of "STEM."
- STEM-infusion means STEM processes are used to teach or practice all content areas, including reading. Thus, reading falls under the umbrella of the word "infusion."
- I am definitely not talking about "pure STEM" in this book. I am by no means a scientist, technologist, engineer, or mathematician. In fact, I was extremely intimidated by the idea of STEM when I first heard about it because of my lack of expertise in the complexity of each of those subjects. Now, I hold those subjects in high regard but instead of feeling intimidated by them, I have drawn out some of their most brain-stretching components and processes and combined them to teach elementary school.

- There are some elements of thematic instruction in STEM. In fact, one of the approaches that will be discussed in Chapter 6 is a thematic approach to STEM-integration. However, STEM-infusion takes thematic instruction beyond just connecting ideas by topic; it connects ideas by concepts that show up across content areas and challenges students to combine this conceptual understanding to design a solution to a problem.

This may all still seem a little unclear right now. If so, hold tight! As you begin to read further about how STEM-infusion plays out in the classroom, it will make more sense. In the meantime, enjoy reading about this EC^{4}S^{3}TREAM-ly interesting approach to instruction.

SAID NO ONE EVER

I have a confession to make. I am a Pinterestaholic. It started out completely innocent. I was legitimately using Pinterest to find lesson ideas, home decorating tips, and healthy recipes (that I will probably never actually cook). But somehow along the way I discovered the Humor category. And the rest is history. From that point on, my Pinteresting was no longer productive. Those little cartoons with the sarcastic yet truthful sayings make me laugh every time. And perhaps my favorite Pinterest jokes are the Said No One Ever ones. Look them up! If you have not figured it out already, I am an easy laugh. But for some reason at the end of an exhausting day, a good Said No One Ever joke is just what I need. And so as I was outlining this chapter, this thought popped into my head:

> I really feel I can easily fit everything I need to accomplish into my school day and every student will receive the individualized help he or she needs.
>
> —Said No One Ever

SPIRALING DOWN

Over the past couple of years, I have received many emails from teachers who are looking to add STEM to their elementary classroom and are searching for lesson plans to get them started. I had the same struggle when I started teaching STEM. If you are brand new to the idea of STEM in elementary school, the energizer type activities found online—such as the classic bridge building challenge—provide a good jumping-off point. Using these, teachers can begin relinquishing their role as the center of the classroom and turn over the reins of leadership to the students. In turn, the students can practice communication and collaboration.

However, after spending some time with these pre-planned activities, you might notice the engineering challenges found online may offer only a loose correlation to your curriculum. For example, probably the most well-known engineering challenge is the egg drop challenge. In this activity, students are asked to design something to protect an egg so it can fall from a certain distance without being broken. The egg drop offers a fantastic opportunity for students to learn the engineering design process as they test and improve their prototype. They also practice the **21st century skills** of communication, collaboration, critical thinking, and creativity. However, if you are not reinforcing your curriculum with those skills, it is difficult to justify spending a large amount of time on the activity. Let's be honest . . . Although we, as teachers, would love to provide our students with these rich opportunities to interact with each other and practice important collaborative skills, our students are tested on reading, math, science, and social studies (and many of us now have evaluations and even paychecks tied to those test scores).

So how *do* we fit it all in? How do we cover all of the standards for all of the subject areas, provide intervention for struggling students, offer challenges to stretch those who are above grade level, and make sure all of this happens in such a way that students will retain the information? And it is not enough that they just memorize and recite the material like we did so often in school, they must also be able to apply the information to higher-order thinking tasks. And although most of us appreciate the value of this additional rigor, we barely fit it all in back in the skill and drill days! To top it all off, we are preparing our students for a world we do not feel very comfortable in, a world where digital literacy is just as important as reading, writing, and arithmetic, a world where unlimited information is at your fingertips and application of knowledge is more valuable than retention. Feeling stressed yet? I know I am not the only teacher who has fallen victim to this overwhelming downward spiral of thought.

A BREATH OF FRESH AIR

As you saw in the previous section, we teachers often times have the best of intentions in integrating innovative strategies but get bogged down when the rubber meets the road. For me, STEM-infusion has been a breath of fresh air in the world of educational change. Instead of adding one more thing that I had to fit into the day, with STEM, we have been able to do the following:

- Give students an opportunity to apply information from all content areas, therefore providing a higher-order level of understanding of the curriculum standards.

- Differentiate organically because each student uses his or her **background knowledge** and applies it in such a way as to find an innovative solution. In this way, every student is stretched.

- Create a culture where mistakes are seen as an important part of growth and learning.
- Offer opportunities for students to practice collaboration, communication, creativity, and critical thinking in a way that enriches the curriculum.

MODEL NOT SUBJECT

Elementary STEM is limited when simply viewed as a subject blending science, technology, engineering, and math. Instead, STEM-infusion is a model of teaching using project-based learning with a focus on creative design for problem solving. Because of that, it enriches all content areas, including English and language arts, by allowing students to make deep connections and apply knowledge creatively.

Instead, STEM-infusion is a model of teaching using project-based learning with a focus on creative design for problem solving.

So why is using this model of teaching so beneficial? The best way to explain it is by telling you exactly what I would tell an elementary school student. I challenge you to teach your students these reasons too (understanding that brain growth is highly motivating for students). STEM is good for your brain for two main reasons:

Firstly, it helps your brain muscle by making new connections between brain cells. Just like doing pushups strengthens your arms because you are using your muscles over and over, the paths between your brain cells are strengthened each time you connect them. Those brain cells are called neurons and alone, they are pretty much useless. Your brain works when chemical messages shoot from one neuron to another. The more these messages travel across a certain path, the more quickly and easily they can travel on that path (Bruer, 1999). I tell my students this works just like a path in the woods. The first time you blaze a trail, it is difficult to get through. But the more you walk that trail, the more well worn it becomes. Similarly, the more ways we connect neurons together, the better we can access that information.

In a STEM-infused environment, students have the opportunity to use those brain paths in many different ways. Because all of the curriculum content areas are connected, the students build more brain connections as well. Therefore, STEM is like CrossFit for the brain!

Secondly, STEM-infusion stretches the brain's capacity. Another important thing you need to know about your brain is that the more often you expose it to new things, the more of those connections you will build. STEM provides an excellent opportunity for **productive struggle** because it pushes students to think beyond what they believe they are capable of. STEM challenges are often difficult, but the teacher is able to support the learner by providing background information, using questioning strategies, and presenting challenges in such a way that the struggle is not overwhelming. This strategy of supporting and stretching is what Wood et al. (1976) referred to as **scaffolding**. They explained scaffolding as an "adult controlling those elements of the task that are essentially beyond the learner's capacity, thus permitting him to concentrate upon and complete only those elements that are within his range of competence."

In STEM-infusion, students are constantly bumping up against difficult tasks and then realizing their potential to overcome obstacles.

As you will read more about later in the book, the impact of students believing in their own potential for brain growth is essential to academic success. In STEM-infusion, students are constantly bumping up against difficult tasks and then realizing their potential to overcome obstacles.

WORKING SMARTER

Inevitably, someone is reading this book because the boss said they had to. And you opened it up thinking STEM-infusion was going to add to your already hectic school day. I hope you soon see this is not the case. Instead, STEM-infusion gives you a way to fit it all in but also in a way that does justice to each content area because the students will build a deeper level of understanding through STEM-infusion than through traditional isolated lessons.

In closing this chapter, I need to make one more confession. Before I started this project, I skipped over the introduction or preface of almost every book I read. I now understand how much I was missing! (To every author I've ever read, I'm sorry!) But reading this book without the preface is going to leave some gaps. So if you are one of those people, who like me, never knew the value of a preface, please go back and read it.

Discussion Starters

- How does STEM enhance the social studies lesson described in this chapter?

- How is STEM-infusion similar and different from pure STEM?

- What challenges in your classroom might STEM-infusion help solve?

- What are the benefits and challenges to systematically teaching the 21st century skills of communication, collaboration, critical thinking, and creativity?

- When have you offered students the opportunity for "productive struggle" in the past? What results have you seen?

YOUR NEXT STEP

Explain to your kiddos how their brains work using the explanations found in this chapter. Throughout the week, ask students to give examples of ways that they are conditioning and stretching their brain muscle!

CHAPTER 2

Why STEM in Elementary?

THEN AND NOW

When I was a little girl, can you guess what I wanted to be when I grew up? Yep! I wanted to be a teacher. When I got home from school, I would go to my grandparents' house and make my very patient granddaddy sit on the side of the guest bed with a bed tray on his lap, as if he were sitting at a desk. I would teach him letter sounds, and how to blend letters into words, and the combinations of letters that made an exception. I wrote out math problems and graded his papers with a fat, red marker. I taught him the names of the planets (back when there were nine of them). And I told him stories from my history book (never realizing he had lived through some of those stories on the beaches of Normandy during World War II because he never talked about that). He faithfully sat and "learned" everything I had learned at school that day. Even at the end of my granddaddy's life, when Alzheimer's disease had taken hold and he did not remember my name anymore, he called me his "school teacher." And for years after that, I dreamed of what it would be like to be a real teacher.

But in all those dreams, I never imagined it would be like this. As a little girl in Grandaddy's guest room, I envisioned myself teaching in the front of the room, writing on the board with kids in rows. I dreamed of making assignments and knowing exactly what I expected my kids to produce in return. I dreamed of teaching my students the same things I had been taught. I had no idea I would teach in a world where most of the knowledge on earth is available from the Internet on the phone I carry in my pocket. I could not have dreamed of a classroom where all of my students have their own iPad. It never occurred to me that the information I was taught in school would be only the baseline of knowledge I provided for my students to build innovative solutions to real-world problems. The idea of a classroom with the constant hum of collaboration is so different from my childhood experience of silent seatwork. And yet, that is the progress education has made in the past quarter of a century.

We must prepare kids to be successful in an unknown future and to actively participate in the building of that future.

And you know what? The dreams our kids have inside their heads represent only a shadow of the future careers they will have too! None of us can imagine the future our kids will live in. Some will have jobs that do not exist yet. Others will have existing professions but with unfathomable technology they will help invent. This is exactly why STEM-infusion is essential for elementary-school kids. We must prepare kids to be successful in an unknown future and to actively participate in the building of that future. And because we do not know what that future looks like, our only course of action is to raise problem-solvers, collaborators, innovators, and risk-takers.

21st CENTURY READINESS

The Partnership for 21st Century Skills has identified four "learning and innovation skills" that are essential for the 21st century workforce: creativity, critical thinking, communication, and collaboration. According to its website, "Learning and innovation skills increasingly are being recognized as the skills that separate students who are prepared for increasingly complex life and work environments in the 21st century, and those who are not." Let's break that statement apart and see how it applies to an elementary STEM-infused classroom.

"Learning and Innovation . . ."

Elementary STEM-infusion gives students constant opportunity to foster each one of these skills:

- **Creativity.** In each design challenge, students use their existing knowledge to come up with a creative solution to a problem. Their ideas must be original, well thought out, and flexible in response to the outcomes of their testing. Because students must test and improve their design several times within a challenge, they are constantly exercising their creativity.

- **Critical Thinking.** It does the students little good in terms of preparing them for their future if we just teach them the facts listed within our standards. They could find those online. Instead, we have to teach them to apply their learning to new and unpredictable circumstances. In a STEM-infused classroom, the teacher is constantly providing the students with authentic scenarios to which students have to apply their content knowledge. Student misconceptions become evident when an idea does not work and students are given the opportunity to self-correct as they improve.

- **Communication and Collaboration.** In a STEM-infused classroom, students are sharing more than they are silent. This type of classroom stands on the principle that students have more to learn from each other than they can learn from the teacher. Therefore, throughout the day, students will be discussing, debating, presenting, blogging, emailing, web chatting, etc. to gain and distribute the information they use and gather throughout their day. As you will see in Chapter 9, the teacher must demonstrate, foster, and scaffold communication and collaboration skills in order to maximize their effectiveness.

"Separate Those Who Are Prepared . . . and Those Who Are Not"

In his book *World Class Learners: Educating Creative and Entrepreneurial Students,* Yong Zhao criticizes the educational paradigm, which dominates most societies, that says we are only preparing students with skills that help them fit in to the current society. This type of education was useful in mass-producing workers for an industrial economy, but that is not the type of economy we live in. Because of **globalization** and technology, our kids will not grow up in a world where industry dominates American economy. That ship has sailed . . . literally . . . as many industrial jobs have moved overseas. But he goes on to say that "America's success in creativity is the outcome of its ineffectiveness in forcing conformity and standardization" (Zhao, 2012). In other words, the United States continues to excel at innovation. And innovation is what will allow our students to compete in a technology-rich, global society.

A STEM-infused elementary classroom cultivates creativity instead of conformity.

A STEM-infused elementary classroom cultivates creativity instead of conformity. In these classrooms, students practice thinking skills instead of rote memorization of a list of standards. This style of learning will serve our students well as we consider the following statement made by Andreas Schleicher, OECD education directorate:

> We live in a fast-changing world, and producing more of the same knowledge and skills will not suffice to address the challenges of the future. A generation ago, teachers could expect that what they taught would last their students a lifetime. Today, because of rapid economic and social change, schools have to prepare students for jobs that have not yet been created, technologies that have not yet been invented and problems that we don't yet know will arise. (Schleicher, 2010)

". . . Increasingly Complex Life and Work Environments . . ."

According to Dr. James Appleberry, president of the American Association of State Colleges and Universities,

> The sum total of humankind's knowledge doubled between 1750 and 1900. It doubled again between 1900 and 1950, again from 1950 to 1960, again from 1960 to 1965. It's been estimated that the sum total of humankind's knowledge has doubled at least every five years since then. It's been further projected that by the year 2020, knowledge or information will double every 73 days. (Appleberry, 2000)

Can you imagine? In just a few years, the amount of knowledge that exists in the whole wide world will double almost two-and-a-half times during our school year! How in the world can we prepare kids with a knowledge base to live, succeed, and contribute in a world like that? Well, teaching them a list of standards written several years ago certainly will not be enough. If we want our kids ready for these increasingly complex work environments, we have to teach them to think critically and creatively.

In 2001, Bloom's Taxonomy (Figure 2.1) was updated in an effort to better reflect the importance of creative thinking in the 21st century. Whereas originally, evaluation was seen as the highest level of thinking, Lorin Anderson's team of experts in psychology, instruction, curriculum, and assessment found that creating was the ultimate assimilation of knowledge (Forehand, 2005). In this body of research, creating is defined as "putting elements together to form a coherent or functional whole; reorganizing elements into a new pattern or structure through generating, planning, or producing" (Anderson & Krathwohl, 2001).

Dr. Willard Daggett and the International Center for Leadership took this concept a step further with their Rigor/Relevance Framework® (Figure 2.2). They asserted that effective teaching not only challenges students to work in the highest levels of the Knowledge Taxonomy (resulting in **rigor**) but also in the deepest level of the Application Model (resulting in **relevance**). The application continuum begins with knowledge of one discipline and stretches to application in one discipline, application across disciplines, application to predictable real-world situations, and finally application to unpredictable real-world situations (Daggett, 2014). In other

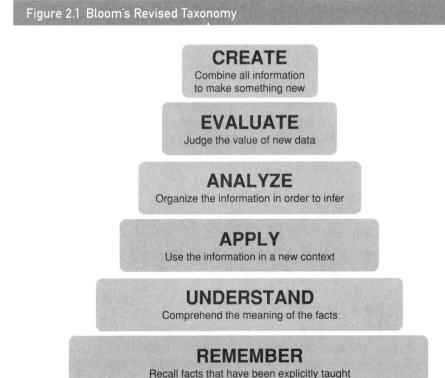

Figure 2.1 Bloom's Revised Taxonomy

CREATE
Combine all information to make something new

EVALUATE
Judge the value of new data

ANALYZE
Organize the information in order to infer

APPLY
Use the information in a new context

UNDERSTAND
Comprehend the meaning of the facts

REMEMBER
Recall facts that have been explicitly taught

Figure 2.2 Rigor/ Relevance Framework®

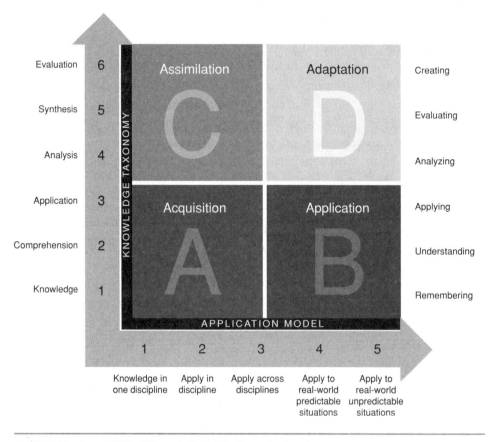

SOURCE: Courtesy of Willard Daggett, EdD, http://www.leadered.com.

words, the most effective type of education is one in which students are pulling together and reorganizing information from all content areas in order to find a solution to an unpredictable real-world problem.

MOTIVATING CHANGE

As you read on through this book, I hope you will see the previous information in this chapter as a foundation for all of the other information. This research has come to me in pieces in the form of professional development activities, conference keynotes, Professional Learning Communities (PLC) discussions, articles, and degree coursework over the past few years. They have assimilated in my brain as elementary STEM-infusion. This information about the mystical future world our kids will grow up in has motivated me to change how I teach and stretch my own imagination and comfort to allow kids the freedom to create. Most likely, if you are still reading, you believe this change is needed too. So how do we do it? We STEM-infuse.

The President's Council of Advisors on Science and Technology lifted up the need for more STEM education in its 2010 report to the president titled "Prepare and Inspire: K–12 Education in Science, Technology, Engineering, and Math [STEM] for America's Future" (President's Council, 2010). The recommendations of this report included the following:

> *This information about the mystical future world our kids will grow up in has motivated me to change how I teach and stretch my own imagination and comfort to allow kids the freedom to create.*

- Showing national support for the state-led movement toward shared standards

- Recruiting and training 100,000 STEM teachers in the next decade

- Creating the STEM Masters Teaching Corps to recognize the best STEM teachers

- Creating a support system for educational technology innovation

- Creating opportunities for students outside the classroom

- Creating 1,000 STEM-focused schools over the next decade

- Ensuring national leadership for STEM education

With STEM being lifted up as a matter of national importance, it is essential that we prioritize it within our classrooms, even our elementary classrooms.

Discussion Starters

- What information in this chapter was most surprising to you? Why?

- What challenges might our students face in their future jobs that have not been an issue in the past?

- In what ways do you feel your current standards prepare students for their futures? In what ways do they fall short?

- In what ways are you preparing your students to help build the unknown future talked about in this chapter?

- What is a lesson that you recently taught in which you required a standard outcome? How could you change the lesson so that the student outcome was unpredictable?

YOUR NEXT STEP

Analyze a lesson plan that you recently taught. Highlight parts in which you are preparing students for an unknown future with skills such as communication, collaboration, creativity, and critical thinking. Circle parts that require tasks based on the assumption that our future economy will look like the present or even the past.

CHAPTER 3

Rigor Meets Relevance

EXPLOSION

Last year, I accidentally sent a first-grade girl home from school with pink hair. The kids had been asking all year for us to make a volcano and several times I had blown them off, stating that the baking soda and vinegar model of a volcano was not scientifically accurate. I had explained to them that although the volcano would look neat, it didn't do much to help them understand landforms.

In the spring, after the 1,423rd time being asked (first graders can be quite ~~obsessive~~ persistent), I decided a volcano demonstration was very important to the students and I should therefore try to work it in to some type of lesson. At that time, students were learning about compare and contrast in their reading class, and I decided it would be helpful to support that concept through a STEM-infused lesson in the STEM lab.

At the time, I had a student teacher and so together we planned two volcano experiences (see Figure 3.1)—a baking soda and vinegar volcano model and a virtual tour of an erupting volcano on their iPads (using an app called Volcano 360). The plan was for the students to experience both and then create a

Figure 3.1 First-grade students observe a classic volcano experiment as part of a language arts compare-and-contrast lesson.

SOURCE: Photo by Linda Talley.

diagram to compare and contrast the two experiences in the Popplet app (see Resource B).

The first few classes we did this activity with went off without a hitch. The students excitedly watched the volcano erupt with me and then enthusiastically enjoyed the virtual experience with the student teacher. However, with the fourth class, things went a little differently. When I poured the vinegar into the volcano, there was only a very small reaction. The students encouraged me to pour more and willfully supporting their first grade logic, I tipped the beaker of vinegar and red food coloring up and poured it into the volcano. Where before the liquid had oozed out of the volcano, it now shot straight out putting a dark pink stripe up the white dress and light-blond hair of an adorable first-grade girl. Apparently, the hole had been blocked and the pressure had built up to unblock it. (Coincidentally, this turned out to be a perfect teachable moment, as this accident was caused by something much more like what actually causes a volcano to erupt.)

EMOTIONAL RELEVANCE

Obviously, this little activity turned out to be even more memorable than expected for those kiddos. And fortunately, Murphy's Law sometimes works to our advantage when providing students with rich, memorable experiences. According to Dr. Kenneth Wesson, "Emotionally charged events consistently enjoy a higher probability of being converted into memories that get permanently stored in the cerebral cortex due to their affective importance." This is why, for example, you are able to remember exactly where you were on September 11, 2001.

That day when the volcano exploded all over the STEM lab, we all sucked in our breath, stared wide-eyed at the pink-striped little girl, and waited for her reaction. And when she cracked a smile, we all burst into laughter. Suddenly, the children had a solid memory that would stick in their heads for years to come. And all I had to do was tie that memory to the concept of compare and contrast so the academic benefit of that pink mess extended beyond a hilarious experience.

MAKING IT MATTER

Not every activity can be emotionally charged in the way the volcano was. However, we as teachers must still find a way to connect our content to something that matters to the student. Do you ever remember asking your teacher, "Why are we doing this?" Have your students asked you that? Students are not likely to invest too much in a topic they feel is only important enough to memorize for a test. They want to see the relevance of a topic beyond the classroom. STEM-infusion is an awesome solution to this problem. When you present students with a real-world problem in which they have to design a solution using their content knowledge, they suddenly have a strong connection to the curriculum. In fact, they become so invested in solving the problem, they do not even realize how completely they are understanding the content.

Students are not likely to invest too much in a topic they feel is only important enough to memorize for a test. They want to see the relevance of a topic beyond the classroom.

For example, with Christmas approaching, I assigned a group of third-grade students the following challenge: *You are a packaging engineer in charge of designing a new package for shipping candy canes.* (See Resource C.) As part of this challenge the students had to do the following:

- Watch a video on packaging engineers and the things they have to consider when designing a package, such as visual aesthetic, environmental concerns, cost of production, cost to consumers, and effectively protecting the product. Then, they developed their own rubric to evaluate their packaging based on this criteria.

- Read an article on how candy canes were made and use the information within it as evidence to defend their package design.

- Calculate the cost of producing their package and the additional cost it would mean for consumers purchasing the product.

- Pitch their packaging solution to a candy cane company using iMovie, Green Screen, or Adobe Voice apps.

All of these concepts—inferencing, environmental effects, defending with evidence, addition and subtraction with money, division, economic impact, and persuasive writing—could have been taught in isolation that week using direct instruction, worksheets, or other more traditional models of instruction. However, the students would not retain the information near as thoroughly as they did. Because they were excited about the outcome of their project—producing the most effective package—they worked diligently to excel in each of the aforementioned skills.

As discussed in the previous chapter, Dr. Willard Daggett emphasized the importance of making content relevant for students (Daggett, 2014). Imagine, for example, I was planning a lesson to teach my students how to defend an idea with evidence from a text. Let's examine how this might look at each of Daggett's levels of relevance (see Table 3.1).

Table 3.1 Daggett's Levels of Relevance

Level 1	**Knowledge in One Discipline**	Students read text. Teacher gives students a conclusion to defend. Students highlight evidence in text to defend conclusion.
Level 2	**Application in One Discipline**	Students read text. Students draw their own conclusion. Students find evidence within the passage to defend their conclusion.
Level 3	**Interdisciplinary Application**	Students read text. Students draw a conclusion. Students do a science experiment to gain evidence to defend their conclusion.
Level 4	**Real-World Predictable Situation**	Students do an interdisciplinary project in which they apply defending a conclusion with evidence but the teacher knows exactly how the project will turn out—in fact all groups' final product will look the same.
Level 5	**Real-World Unpredictable Situation**	Students do an interdisciplinary project in which they apply defending a conclusion with evidence and have the autonomy to take the project in many different directions. The student outcome could look very different depending on how the students apply their knowledge but an authentic application of the skill has been used.

SOURCE: **Levels and descriptors from Daggett (2014).**

The candy cane lesson above is an example of a Level 5 relevance activity. The students apply their understanding of defending a conclusion with evidence by creating their own original solution to a real-world problem and then defending it. Not only that, but they are also practicing an abundance of other skills across content areas.

THE RELEVANCE TRAP

At this point, I offer a word of caution. When creating STEM-infused lesson plans, relevance is the easy part. However, it is easy to get caught up in the excitement of planning STEM-infused lessons that increase student engagement but forget the other half of Daggett's framework—rigor. Admittedly, this is a mistake I myself have made over the past couple of years. In creating and implementing lessons for an elementary STEM lab, I have gotten excited about the overwhelming student engagement but neglected the learning outcomes. Don't get me wrong—student engagement is an essential part of good teaching. But I fear, at times, I have sacrificed rigor for relevance. The two are not mutually exclusive. In fact, the art of strong pedagogy is finding the sweet spot where students are so engaged they embrace challenges that push them to apply their understanding at a deeper level.

In fact, the art of strong pedagogy is finding the sweet spot where students are so engaged they embrace challenges that push them to apply their understanding at a deeper level.

One of the most important considerations when developing rigorous lessons is setting strong objectives from the very beginning of the learning process. Recently, I was helping a teacher plan a science lesson on physical and chemical changes. Although we had identified an engaging science experiment for the students, we felt the students needed more explicit instruction about facts related to these topics. We decided to create a Padlet wall with links to websites and videos that would provide the necessary information. Although all the information would be disseminated to students, the links themselves did not provide an opportunity for productive academic struggle. Therefore, we decided to create a task for students to complete for each link that provided them with more challenge.

When creating these tasks, we wanted to make sure students were considering answers to higher-order questions. We used a Bloom's Taxonomy diagram (see Figure 2.1, page 15) to help us create a rubric to establish student learning goals for each task. In grading students' responses, we were able to screenshot evidence to justify our evaluation of each task. Again, this activity began with a simple science experiment and research tool but was transformed into a much more rigorous learning experience by focusing on higher-order outcomes and integration of content areas based on cross-cutting concepts.

Just like we did with the relevance example before, let's look back at what our lesson on defending a conclusion with evidence might look like at each stage of rigor according to Bloom's Revised Taxonomy (see Table 3.2).

From my perspective in elementary STEM, providing engaging, memorable, and meaningful learning opportunities for our students in the **Common Core State Standards** era is quite exciting. There is no question that neat apps and interactive projects make content more relevant and enjoyable for students. However, in using these, we cannot forget the pitfalls we learned from the whole learner movement. A lack of rigor is what led us to standards-focused instruction in the first place. Exciting classroom experiences that lack opportunities for students to analyze,

Table 3.2 Bloom's Revised Taxonomy

Level 1	**Remembering**	Teacher models defending a conclusion with evidence and then assesses the students doing the same thing on the same passage. Students are expected to draw the same conclusions as the teacher and support it with the same evidence.
Level 2	**Understanding**	Teacher models defending a conclusion with evidence but then assesses students doing the same thing on a different passage. Teacher identifies the conclusion and asks students to defend it.
Level 3	**Applying**	Students read a passage and draw their own conclusion and then defend it with evidence from the passage.
Level 4	**Analyzing**	Students read several sources in order to draw a conclusion and then compile a defense using evidence from many sources.
Level 5	**Evaluating**	Students do an experiment with a predictable outcome as research to provide evidence to support a conclusion.
Level 6	**Creating**	Students create their own original solution to a problem and then defend their solution with evidence from their cycle of design and improvement.

SOURCE: Levels and descriptors from Forehand (2005).

evaluate, and synthesize information are likely to yield basic-level understanding at best and educational gaps at worst.

Every lesson could be taught in a million different ways. The art of teaching is deciding what approach will give the students the most meaningful, lasting connection to the content. It also means providing opportunity for productive struggle because that stretches students in a way that prepares them for more than just understanding the concepts. It prepares them for their unpredictable future. For the sake of our students, let's find a balance between relevance and rigor. For me, STEM-infusion has provided that bridge.

THE ROLE OF TECHNOLOGY

Although digital technology is one of the primary components of STEM, you will notice that I do not devote major portions of this book to a specific mention of the subject. This is because I know firsthand how digital technology in the elementary classroom can be misused. In the same way that STEM-infusion projects can easily turn into high relevance with low rigor, digital technology projects can do the same. When we began our first year of one-to-one iPads at our school, we were careful to promote apps used for creativity instead of consumption. By doing this, we intended for students to utilize their device to innovate, not to play games or practice skill-and-drill activities. However, what we noticed is that in some classrooms, students were producing work that they could have done before any teaching took place. In other words, there were no student learning outcomes other than learning to use the technology itself.

Several months into school after a round of observations, our administrators made a statement that refocused us all on the role of digital technology. They said, "If a student could have done that project before you taught the lesson, no rigorous learning has taken place." It seems simple, but it's a mistake teachers make over and over. Educational technology should be used to enhance strong pedagogy, not replace it. Therefore, we have been careful to keep technology in its place to insure a high level of not only relevance but rigor in our classrooms.

This is not to say that explicitly teaching computer skills and digital citizenship is not important. Both are imperative to prepare our students for the world they will live in. Our school has participated in Hour of Code the past two years, our students use Learning.com to develop digital literacy, and many of our teachers start the school day with "Genius Bar," in which they teach specific tech literacy skills. We want our students to be self-sufficient with their devices and literate in a digital society. However, we have to be careful not to allow our devices to dominate our instruction at the expense of relevance.

- Describe a time when you have had a happy accident or teachable moment in your classroom. How have you used the emotions of the moment to solidify knowledge for your students?

- What topics have been difficult to answer the "why are we doing this" question on in the past? How might STEM-infusion help you answer that question?

- When have you felt rigor suffered for the purpose of relevance or vice versa?

- In this chapter, the author describes using Bloom's Taxonomy verbs when building a rubric. In what ways do you intentionally write rigor into your lesson plans?

YOUR NEXT STEP

Identify a lesson that you recently taught in which students were highly motivated, but academic rigor could be improved. Do a web search for "Bloom's verbs" and choose a list of verbs associated with each level of Bloom's Taxonomy. Use the verbs in the Analyze, Evaluate, and Create sections to rewrite your objectives for that lesson.

OR

Identify a lesson in which students achieved rigorous interaction with the content but did not necessarily connect with the subject matter on a meaningful level. Brainstorm ways in which you could introduce that same content through a real-world, unpredictable situation.

CHAPTER 4

The Cross-Cutting Concepts Approach to STEM-Infusion

THE PATTERN REVELATION

For my first teaching job, I was hired fresh out of undergrad and four days before school would start. I was thrilled when I was given the key to a glorified double-wide (which we later deemed a "learning cottage"). With a classroom stuffed full of desks and my brain stuffed full of idealistic teaching theory, I dove in headfirst to teaching fourth grade. And with so little time for preparations, I gratefully accepted pacing guides from a colleague and began planning lessons for each subject—English/language arts, math, science, and social studies.

About three weeks into school, I was introducing a science lesson on life cycles when a particularly mischievous yet incredibly intelligent boy raised his hand and remarked, "Mrs. Reagan, you sure do love teaching about cycles, don't you? It seems like that's all we've learned about this year so far."

Thinking this a strange comment since this was the first time I had mentioned the word *cycle* all year long, I responded, "What do you mean?"

Mr. Mischievously Intelligent replied, "Well, today you are teaching us about life cycles in science, and before that, we were talking about ecosystems which are basically like a giant cycle because everything depends on each other and it's a never ending circle of one thing affecting another. In math, we've been learning about problem-solving, which is really just a cycle too. One piece of the cycle is missing and you have to use the other pieces to figure out what goes there. And of course, we've already talked in social studies about how history repeats itself. And in reading, we've talked a lot about drawing conclusions, which is the same as math problem solving . . . we're just looking for word clues instead of number clues to fill in the cycle."

Huh . . . out of the mouths of babes.

And thus, before a professor in my masters program taught me about strengthening neuron connections and before the Common Core Standards drafting committee had discussed cross-cutting concepts, a ten-year-old enlightened me about the genius of helping students see all content in terms of patterns.

I can assure you that moment was the quietest that tiny classroom was all year long as every kid, my assistant, and I all sat trying to digest this remarkable revelation. And thus, before a professor in my masters program taught me about strengthening neuron connections and before the Common Core Standards drafting committee had discussed **cross-cutting concepts**, a ten-year-old enlightened me about the genius of helping students see all content in terms of patterns. Although it would be several years before I began using STEM-infusion to accomplish this goal, that boy changed the way I approached lesson planning. Thank you, Mr. Mischievously Intelligent!

CROSS-CUTTING CONCEPTS

As you read in Chapter 1, true STEM-infusion is accomplished by creating lesson plans that enrich the curriculum of all content areas in the elementary classroom. In the past couple of years, the teachers I work with and I have developed three different approaches to creating STEM-infused lesson plans. Chapters 4 through 6 will explain each of these approaches, how to implement them, and what classroom style lends itself best to each approach.

The first approach, the cross-cutting concepts approach to STEM-Infusion, was inspired by the aforementioned ten-year-old. In this approach, a teacher begins by identifying concepts that appear in some form in standards from various content areas. *A Framework for K–12 Science Education: Practices, Core Ideas, and Crosscutting Concepts* explains, "Crosscutting concepts have value because they provide students with connections and intellectual tools that are related across the differing areas of disciplinary content and can enrich their application of practices and their understanding of core ideas" (National Research Council, 2012, p. 233). In other words, these are ideas that appear across the curriculum—in English/language arts, math, science, and social studies. Chapter 4 of *Framework* identifies seven of these concepts as follows:

- Patterns
- Cause and effect
- Scale, proportion, and quantity
- Systems and system models
- Energy and matter
- Structure and function
- Stability and change

In looking at these cross-cutting concepts, also referenced in the Next Generation Science Standards, along with the Common Core State Standards for English/language arts and mathematics and our state's social studies standards, I have noticed many additional concepts that appear across the curriculum:

- Citing evidence/defending
- Inferring/drawing conclusions
- Compare and contrast
- Cause and effect
- Risk taking
- Modeling
- Problem/solution

- Making connections
- Multiple meaning words
- Point of view/perspective taking
- Questioning/what if?
- Design/redesign
- Analysis
- Sequencing
- Cycles

CREATING STEM-INFUSED LESSON PLANS WITH CROSS-CUTTING CONCEPTS

To take a **cross-cutting concepts approach** to STEM-infusion, begin by looking at all your standards and grouping them according to cross-cutting concepts. One team of teachers I met with wrote their standards on sticky notes then stuck them on poster boards labeled with a cross-cutting concept. Patterns will begin to emerge and the concepts become umbrellas under which you teach certain skills. For example, a kindergarten teacher might choose cause and effect as one of his or her umbrellas. As part of that unit, the teacher might teach fact families in math, drawing conclusions and character interactions in reading, wellness in science, and community in social studies. All of these topics reinforce the idea that one factor affects another.

After deciding on a concept and the standards that will be taught under it, the next step is to write an essential question for the unit. An essential question should be broad enough that there are multiple ways of answering it so that various parts of the unit will lend evidence to answering the question. In the cause and effect example above, the question might be, "How can one person affect the whole community?"

Next, the teacher creates a design challenge that allows the students to apply knowledge from all content areas that lends itself to answering the essential question. This is where teachers have to get really creative. If you search "STEM challenge for kindergarten on cause and effect," few results will turn up. Instead, think about where the concept shows up in the real world. What are some real challenges your students face relating to cause and effect? Some of these might include the effects of littering, the causes of germ spreading, the effects of danger on the playground, the consequences for neglecting chores, balancing homework and outside time, or the effects of random acts of kindness. By choosing topics that are relevant to students, they will have the background knowledge to begin thinking innovatively to solve the challenge. For the purpose of this example, we will use the following germ-spreading scenario.

One student comes to school sick. What might happen to the class by the end of the day? Why would that happen? With your group, design a solution to keep it from happening. (See Resource D.)

Once a design challenge is chosen, the teachers' lesson plans can vary greatly. Some teachers continued teaching their daily lessons on the standards being taught within that umbrella in the way they taught them before STEM-infusion. However, they emphasized the umbrella topic throughout instruction. For example, the teacher might teach fact families using counters but discuss with the children the cause of a number getting larger is adding more to it and the effect is taking some away from it. The teacher simply embeds the cross-cutting concept into his or her vocabulary during instruction. Doing this effectively accomplishes the goal of helping students make connections.

Other teachers make an even stronger connection between the weekly design challenge and daily skill instruction. In the example above, the teacher might create relevant math tasks or word problems related to the germ-spreading scenario:

Twenty kids came to school, but three of them went home sick. How many students were still at school? (Seventeen.) *What was the effect of three kids*

Figure 4.1 Kindergarten students explore solutions to the germ-spreading problem.

SOURCE: Photo by Linda Talley.

going home? (There were fewer students in the class.) *What may have caused the students to get sick?* (Students were spreading germs by not washing hands, not covering their mouths when they cough, shaking hands, etc.) (See Figure 4.1.)

Either way, the students will understand the concept of cause and effect better because the teacher has helped connect the dots across subject areas. This is no longer a topic specific to literature, but the students now see how it applies to math, science, social studies, and, most importantly, *their real lives.*

CONCERNS ABOUT REARRANGING STANDARDS

When talking about rearranging standards, this concern is always brought up—"There are some standards that HAVE to be taught in a certain order. They build on each other and therefore cannot be rearranged." This is absolutely true and legitimate, especially in math. I suggest continuing to teach the math concept standards in the proper order. However, you can reinforce the process standards through STEM-infused projects aligned with cross-cutting concepts. Furthermore, if you are looking, you can usually find some type of connection between a math concept and concepts in other disciplines. Ask the students! They can help you find the connection.

WHEN TO USE THIS APPROACH

This approach to STEM-infusion works best in a school that allows a high level of teacher autonomy. In order to go this route, teachers must have the flexibility to rearrange their pacing guides in such a way that helps the students make connections. Furthermore, the administration must have a high level of confidence in its teachers in order to trust that every standard will get covered with the appropriate amount of rigor. It is a risk, but I have found the depth of understanding students build is retained much better than when the concepts are taught in isolation.

It is a risk, but I have found the depth of understanding students build is retained much better than when the concepts are taught in isolation.

Discussion Starters

- Choose one of the cross-cutting concepts listed in the chapter. Make a list of as many of your standards or topics as possible that would fit into that concept. (If not a self-contained classroom, work with teachers in other disciplines to make your list.)

- How would the cross-cutting concepts approach to STEM-infusion enhance your instruction?

- What are some of the challenges of this approach to STEM-infusion?

- A solid and thorough understanding of the content being taught is foundational in using this approach. How can you support new teachers in developing cross-cutting conceptual lessons?

YOUR NEXT STEP

Choose one of the cross-cutting concepts listed in this chapter. Find standards in two different content areas that can fit under the umbrella of that concept. Brainstorm a design challenge in which your students connect the information in those two disciplines to the cross-cutting concept.

CHAPTER 5

The Standards Alignment Approach to STEM-Infusion

OPERATION TOP SECRET MESSAGE

When I applied for my job as a STEM lab teacher, I decided to invite my building level and district administrators into my fourth-grade classroom to see me teach. I figured it would give me a leg up if they saw I was already using STEM-type lessons in my classroom to integrate our curriculum. Let me describe the scene they saw when they walked into my classroom on that late winter morning. All of the desks were pushed back against the walls, revealing a vast open space in the middle of the room where groups of students were clustered. A quick tour around the room revealed students building paper airplanes, zip lines, sling shots, pulley systems, etc. out of materials such as yarn, paper, rubber bands, paper clips, and other office products (see Figure 5.1). And then there was the icing on the cake . . . me standing on the counter in a tutu and tiara with a trifold project board decorated to look like a castle around me. In front of me was an expanse of blue butcher paper sprinkled with glitter and a stuffed alligator in the middle. I figured they would either think I was crazy or just extremely committed to STEM. (Turns out, I was both!)

Figure 5.1 Fourth-grade students design slingshots, pulleys, zip lines, etc. to get a top-secret message to Princess Reagan.

SOURCE: Photo by Linda Talley.

The activity happening in this strange scene was Operation Top Secret Message, which to this day is my favorite STEM-infused activity of all time (see Resource E). At the time, I was teaching author's purpose in language arts, reducing fractions in math, and forces and motion in science. I wanted to come up with a challenge that would be both memorable yet reinforce all three of these unrelated concepts. Therefore, I challenged the students to write a secret message and somehow get it to me, Princess Reagan, who was trapped in a tower.

STARTING WITH THE STANDARDS

In the previous chapter, we built STEM-infused lessons by starting with a cross-cutting concept and pulling in all of the standards that could fall under that umbrella. However, there are times when there are just certain standards you need to teach or reinforce at the same time. Therefore, instead of taking the cross-cutting concepts approach described in the previous chapter, you want to take the **standards-based approach** to STEM-infusion. With this approach, the teacher

This takes some creativity on the part of the teacher and some imagination on the part of the students, but it definitely gives the students an opportunity to connect otherwise unrelated concepts in their minds.

looks at all of the standards being taught at the time and creates a design challenge where all of the standards are practiced. This takes some creativity on the part of the teacher and some imagination on the part of the students, but it definitely gives the students an opportunity to connect otherwise unrelated concepts in their minds. Here is a description of how Operation Top Secret Message brought three unrelated concepts together.

- **Language Arts.** The students read an article on a controversial topic. They then had to write a persuasive letter defending their opinion on the matter, but instead of handing in their persuasive writing sample, they had to solve a little design challenge to get it to me.

- **Science.** The students had to use the science vocabulary from our forces and motion unit—gravity, inertia, point of reference, speed, force, friction, etc.—in their discussion as they figured out some type of contraption that would allow them to get the secret message to Princess Reagan in the tower.

- **Math.** The students were given a limited number of each material to work with. Throughout the challenge, they had to document what fraction (in lowest terms) of each material had been used in their project.

CONNECTING THE UNCONNECTED

In 2012, I had the pleasure of hearing Dr. Kenneth Wesson, neuroscientist and expert on brain-considerate learning, speak at the National Science Teachers Association (NSTA) STEM forum. During his keynote, he made two interesting points that form a basis for this approach to STEM-infusion.

- "Our academic curriculum should reflect the beauty of *patterns* that blend together, rather than resembling a *patchwork* of unrelated content and experiences. Patterns are easy to process, comprehend, and remember because of the blended relationships" (Wesson, 2012).

- "As brain cells develop into networks, the brain makes no distinction between the academic disciplines" (Wesson, 2012).

In other words, the brain learns better when things are connected together. However, there is no biological need for these things to be naturally connected in terms of disciplines. Our brain is not naturally categorized into sections by academic content area—math, language arts, science, etc. The patterns in our brain are organized based on the way the information was input. Therefore, the more ways we connect content in our students' brains, the more avenues they have to track that information down during recall. Thus, we can help students form a connection by presenting unrelated material in an interconnected project.

The patterns in our brain are organized based on the way the information was input.

WHEN TO USE THIS APPROACH

This approach to STEM-infusion is the one that I see used most often. Its main advantage is not having to move standards around to fit your projects. Instead, you make your projects fit your standards. Therefore, it creates an authentic connection between ideas that are otherwise unrelated.

This is especially helpful if you work in a school where you are required to follow a set pacing guide. With an emphasis on teaching with **fidelity**, many administrators are likely to accept STEM-infusion as a method for instructing only when it follows the prescribed pacing. This is a legitimate concern and therefore, this approach can provide a solution. This approach allows you to teach and practice the skills prescribed but in a way that helps students form connections between those unrelated skills.

BRAINSTORMING PROJECT IDEAS

The most difficult thing about this approach to STEM-infusion is coming up with project ideas. Because the skills we are teaching are not yet connected in our own brains, it is difficult for us as teachers to come up with a project that relates them together. So often my colleagues say, "I really want to plan STEM-infused lessons, but I just have trouble coming up with project ideas." Here are a few pieces of advice I give in response to this statement:

- Write out your objectives for all the skills you need to include in the project. Honestly, when I was in college, I did not understand the great need for writing out strong objectives on our lesson plans. However, in the past few years I have seen that this discipline is essential to making sure activities will yield rigorous and relevant student outcomes. When planning a STEM-infused activity, there is just something about seeing all of the objectives on paper at the same time. Maybe you can spend your brain energy coming up with a creative challenge to connect them instead of trying to picture several unrelated objectives in your head. I'm not sure. But what I do know is, I am able to think of challenges quicker when looking at all the objectives.

- Start with just two objectives in different content areas (maybe math and science). Once you learn to integrate two subjects into your projects, you can begin pulling in objectives from more content areas.

- Brainstorm in groups. Last year, the first-grade team at our school planned a STEM-infused lesson together every Wednesday afternoon. They would look at the standards they would be teaching the next week, throw out ideas, and build on those ideas together. By the end of the year, these meetings ran like a machine. By the end of a thirty- or forty-five-minute planning session, they would walk away with a fully planned STEM challenge with materials ready. I am a strong believer in synergy—that the sum of our efforts is greater than what we can do individually. If you are planning to get serious about STEM-infusion, it's time to rally a group of teacher friends to dive in with you.

- Consider problems that matter to the kids. I have a colleague who uses the "service learning" model to teach almost everything. At the beginning of the year, the students commit to "being the change they want to see in the world" and brainstorm a list of problems they would like to help change. They've identified everything from hunger in our community to the Ebola outbreak in West Africa. And this brilliant teacher finds ways to tie nearly all of her teaching to these problems her students identify. If you have your students identify a list of problems, you have topics to choose from when trying to tie content together into a STEM challenge.

- Think crazy! Obviously, pure STEM-infusion in its most relevant form calls for challenges that require kids to solve authentic real-world problems. However, I would argue that in the limitless imaginations of our elementary kiddos, STEM challenges where teacher-princesses are trapped in towers are a relevant problem. Therefore, I believe not every single challenge has to be a challenge real engineers are working to solve too. (Although it is great to have some of those.) But let your imagination go wild in coming up with challenges and your students' imagination will go wild trying to solve them.

LET THE CREATIVITY BEGIN

Throughout this book, you will read about many examples of STEM-infused lessons built with the standards-based approach. For example, the candy cane packaging project was designed starting with the standards concerning defending an idea with evidence and persuasive writing (in language arts), money (in math), economy (in social studies), and designing solutions to real world problems (in science). At this point in the book, I would challenge you to plan a STEM challenge integrating at least two standards you are about to teach. Write out your objectives for a couple subjects and toss around ideas of ways those two things could relate. Your very first STEM challenge may not be very involved and that's okay. Some of my third-grade teacher friends had students design a game inspired by Native American culture. They then wrote a "how-to" essay explaining how the game was played. The game had to work and the instructions had to make sense and be accurate. This is a simple activity, but it met the qualifications for STEM-infusion: collaborative, design-based, integrating content areas, unpredictable outcomes, etc. Don't let yourself be intimidated by thinking you have to plan a huge activity involving the entire week's curriculum content the first time. Start with something manageable. And with small successes, your creativity and comfort with STEM-infusion will grow quickly.

Don't let yourself be intimidated by thinking you have to plan a huge activity involving the entire week's curriculum content the first time. Start with something manageable.

- How did you feel as the author described the scene in her classroom at the beginning of the chapter? What is your comfort level with that type of classroom environment?

- As Dr. Kenneth Wesson explained, our brains do not require that information be sorted by academic discipline as it is input into the brain. What implications does this research have for schools that break up the day by subject area?

- How would the standards alignment approach to STEM-infusion enhance your instruction?

- What are some of the challenges of this approach to STEM-infusion?

- Who are the teachers in your building who might be willing to brainstorm project ideas with you?

YOUR NEXT STEP

Choose two standards from different content areas that you are teaching next week. Brainstorm a design challenge in which your students apply both standards while solving the challenge.

CHAPTER 6

The Thematic Approach to STEM-Infusion

PLAY BALL

Recently, I was working with a group of third graders who were reading the story *Roberto Clemente: Pride of the Pittsburgh Pirates* by Jonah Winter in their basal readers. I decided baseball would make a nice theme for a STEM-infused activity (see Resource F). After reading the story, I challenged the students to design a baseball facility for our high school baseball team (using an imaginary $100,000 donation to the program). (This was a somewhat authentic challenge because the team does not currently have its own field. They practice on our school playground and play at the local college field.) The students had a menu of standard and upgrade choices for items to purchase for their facility. (The prices on this sheet were not accurate but were made up for the sake of the challenge.) They were required to budget their $100,000 by prioritizing and selecting items from the list.

As research, the students interviewed one of our assistant coaches to ask questions about the priorities, safety, comfort, etc. for their baseball facility. I was amazed at the insightful questions they asked. After using their subtraction and addition skills to budget their materials, spending as much as possible without going over the limit, the students designed their facility using a painting app. Next, the

Figure 6.1 Third graders give a tour of their virtual baseball facility using the Green Screen app by Do Ink.

SOURCE: Photo by Linda Talley.

students used a green screen (see Figure 6.1) to make it look like they were live inside their drawing of the baseball facility and a teleprompter app to type a persuasive essay on why their facility design was best. The students defended their facility design by giving a tour of the facility.

As part of this activity, the students practiced objectives regarding reading for understanding, creating relevant questions, money math, persuasive writing, public speaking, technology, and collaboration. However, the entire project started out with the theme of baseball, all because of the story the students were reading.

THE THEMATIC APPROACH

The baseball challenge above is an example of the **thematic approach** to STEM-infusion. The thematic approach means taking a theme—perhaps from a story or an event the students are studying in history—and using it as the foundation for planning a STEM-infused lesson. Where the approach in Chapter 4 started with a conceptual umbrella to connect content areas, this approach starts with a thematic one. The first-grade team I mentioned in the previous chapter frequently used the theme from their basal story as the jumping-off point for their STEM challenges. Themes they integrated included school, space, pets, communication, games, and sports. This gave the team a context in which to think of a challenge. Then the team wove in objectives from math, writing, and other content areas to the challenge.

For example, the week they read *Let's Go to the Moon*, a nonfiction text on moon exploration, the first-grade team presented its students with this challenge: Build "arms" for a moon rover that will allow astronauts to collect rocks and other materials from inside the rover (see Resource G). The teacher then created a moon rover by cutting a hole in a tri-fold project display board. The students used cardboard tubes, paper, straws, spoons, masking tape, etc. to build "arms" that could protrude from the board and collect rocks from a pan of sand (see Figure 6.2). This proved more difficult than the teachers expected. The students had to stretch their brains to problem solve when the arm was too long to control, too short to reach, collected too much sand with the rocks, broke off outside the rover, etc.

Instead, the purpose of this activity was to build 21st century learning skills of collaboration, communication, critical thinking, and creativity while also strengthening background knowledge for the story the students were reading.

In this way, the teachers used the story in their reading book as a jumping-off point for the theme of their project. In contrast to the previous two chapters, the goal of this challenge was not to strengthen student understanding of a concept being taught across content areas or to reinforce a specific language, math, science, or social studies standard. Instead, the purpose of

SOURCE: Photo by Linda Talley.

this activity was to build 21st century learning skills of collaboration, communication, critical thinking, and creativity while also strengthening background knowledge for the story the students were reading. Furthermore, the teachers were able to center their math tasks around the space theme as well, in order to tie in other content areas.

NOT YOUR MAMA'S THEMATIC TEACHING

I have heard many teachers who have been in the education business for a couple of decades talk about the swing of the pendulum between rigorous skills-based instruction and a holistic approach to education. In fact, in my own lifetime, as a student and then as a teacher, I have been affected by the 1980s swing toward basics after President Ronald Reagan's *A Nation at Risk* report, then back toward holistic learning in an effort to educate the whole child in the 1990s, followed by the skill-focused No Child Left Behind initiative of the early millennium, and now the Common Core State Standards that have consumed educational debate in the current decade. A web search of the phrase "educational pendulum" results in page after page of opinion pieces written by teachers begging for the swing to stop.

As seems to be human nature, we in the business of education tend to overcorrect in order to improve. In my estimation, there are three major flaws to this line of thinking:

1. **The Problem of Extremes.** I am no expert in statistics, but I do have a basic understanding of the bell-shaped curve. In short, the extremes, whatever they are, do not tend to apply to many people. Thus, it seems to me that the idea of our educational system living in one extreme or the other does not make much sense. When we are teaching at one extreme, we are only reaching students who learn best with that extreme type of teaching. There are some kids who are most successful in a world of skill and drill. And there are others who can thrive in a highly unstructured and creative learning environment. However, most students find their sweet spot somewhere between the two.

2. **Time to Work Out the Kinks.** A ten-year cycle is hardly enough time to create, implement, and fine-tune an educational reform. In fact, it seems that just about the time educators start to understand how to best implement a set of standards or an educational trend, another group has compiled its argument for why it won't work. And therefore, the tides begin to change again in the other direction. Therefore, we spend so much time fixing what's broken, we rarely spend time in improvement. (As a STEM advocate, I assure you this is the most essential step of any design process.)

3. **Reactive Instead of Proactive.** As stated before, the pendulum swing is usually an attempt to fix what is not working in the education world. We look at PISA [Program for International Student Assessment] reports and the global economy and panic because we as a nation don't stack up. In this state of stress, we take an extreme approach to reform. We say, "This isn't working so we must try the exact opposite!" But what if we didn't plan our reforms reactively? Instead of focusing on what's not working and trying to "not do that," we might benefit from looking toward the future. What will our kids need to be successful when they graduate? What will make them productive in the future workforce? I would argue that looking forward would provide us a more balanced set of goals than looking backward.

Obviously, my point in all of this is to say that balance is the answer and I believe STEM-infusion is a legitimate approach to find this balance. My concern when I talk about a thematic approach to STEM-infusion is that people will assume this approach is another extreme swing of the pendulum back toward whole child education. It sounds like the thematic integration we have seen before. However, the version of thematic instruction I am talking about is different. It focuses on an element of problem-solving and higher-order thinking that may not have been as prevalent in the previous version.

WHEN TO USE THIS APPROACH

Many teachers have found that the thematic approach to STEM-infusion is a great first step in trying to integrate STEM into the classroom. This approach fits easily into existing curriculum and does not require the entire pacing guide to be reworked. It can easily be treated as an add-on for classrooms trying to sprinkle in some STEM without completely redesigning the curriculum.

I do feel this approach is as beneficial in helping kids make connections as the other two approaches. Therefore, it is important once you take this first step to eventually move toward one of the other methods in order to deepen STEM-infusion's impact.

It may seem that I have placed these three chapters backward since the conceptual method is the most involved while thematic is a good first step. However, I placed them this way in order to make sure the reader fully understands the big picture: the goal and eventual possibilities of STEM-infusion. However, as we move beyond methods, I would suggest the following process in STEM-infusing your lessons. First, design a lesson using the thematic approach in order to integrate problem-solving into your existing curriculum. This gives students practice in creative thinking and allows the teacher to adjust to his or her new role as facilitator instead of giver of knowledge. When that becomes more comfortable, move to the standards-based approach by designing a challenge that allows kids to practice objectives from various content areas. Finally, transition toward a conceptual approach in which students are connecting important concepts that inform various disciplines. In doing this, you are working toward a more authentic integration of content with the design process.

This gives students practice in creative thinking and allows the teacher to adjust to his or her new role as facilitator instead of giver of knowledge.

Discussion Starters

- In what ways have you felt a pendulum swing in education? How would STEM-infusion help balance those extremes?

- How would the thematic approach to STEM-infusion enhance your instruction?

- What are some of the limitations of this approach to STEM-infusion?

- Which approach to STEM-infusion do you think would work best in your classroom? Why?

YOUR NEXT STEP

Choose a theme from a story you read in class. Design a challenge based on that theme in which students use a combination of science, technology, engineering, and/or math to solve the challenge.

CHAPTER 7

Assessing STEM

THE TESTING MESS

Last year, I took on the adventure of becoming the testing coordinator for my school. As such, I was in charge of scheduling, organizing materials, assigning and training proctors, maintaining test security, and so forth during our two weeks of state testing. After hours of planning and preparing, the start of the first test was, in my mind, a relief. After all the tests were distributed that first day, I thought, "Whew! We made it." This was the first time the office had seemed calm in weeks. But then the phone rang.

Apparently, one of our third graders "got sick" all over his test . . . with one minute and eighteen seconds left before a break. I was relieved to find out we only had to destroy the contaminated test materials, not send them back to the state, as had been the case in previous years. (Yuck! And were they not destroyed already?) But then I found out that because he had completed the test before the "incident," we had to preserve his answers. Meaning the principal and I had the pleasure of rinsing off the answer document in order to move his answers to a new document. Needless to say, this is a day I will never forget and a day I learned a whole new dimension of school leadership.

But all this to say, stakes are high when it comes to assessing what our kids know. Sometimes laughably so. But for all of the controversy that surrounds standardized testing, there is one thing we as teachers need not lose sight of: Assessing our students and meeting their individual needs based on those assessments is about a moral imperative, not a state mandate. In other words, we owe it to our kids to do a good job of keeping check on where they are, to what extent they are meeting goals, and what skill gaps are forming. And then we must provide what they need to extend those skills, fill in gaps, and set new goals.

Assessing our students and meeting their individual needs based on those assessments is about a moral imperative, not a state mandate.

MY MISTAKE

Embarrassingly, I speak from experience when I tell of the importance of **assessment** and the effect a lack of assessment can have on students. During my first year teaching, I just did not understand how to use formative assessment to differentiate based on students' needs. It was not because I had not been taught. I look back at my college program (at a college I still believe has the best teacher ed preparation ever) and now see how my professors carefully emphasized the importance of assessment, building all teaching models around it. However, I just missed the point somehow. I understood it intellectually but not pragmatically. And when it came down to real students, real lesson plans, and real decision making in the classroom, I ended up spending a lot of time teaching to the middle.

My high kids were not stretched to their potential and my low kids did not have their needs met.

Fortunately, what I lacked in assessment I made up for in enthusiasm for learning and relationships that resulted in an ability to motivate students. And, don't get me wrong—those two things can go a long way. But at the end of the year, when my test scores came back, my achievement scores were just fine (because the kids had been a generally bright class overall to start with), but my growth scores were terrible. My kids were smart in spite of the year they spent with me, not because of it. And you may be thinking, "That's just one test. You can't possibly base the success of the year on it." And, honestly, I don't. I still have positive relationships with some of the students and their parents from my first year of teaching, and I absolutely do not stand to discredit the importance of that. However, upon self-reflection, I knew I had missed the boat when it came to formative assessment in order to differentiate. Academically, I could have helped those students grow much more.

ASSESSING STEM

And so in this chapter, I want to offer some ideas for how to assess STEM-infused lessons. However, most of these suggested methods of assessment are not specific to STEM-infusion. These are "testing alternatives" that provide feedback to help inform instruction for any instructional model but work especially well for problem-based learning, STEM-infusion, and other performance learning tasks.

I have found that students can translate the knowledge gained during STEM-infused learning onto traditional tests. In other words, teaching using a STEM-infused model does not retract from a student's ability to perform on a standardized test. However, I have found that standardized tests do not assess the intricate skills a student gains from this type of learning. Therefore, we need ways to assess all skills practiced during a STEM-infused activity—content-specific skills, process skills, interactive skills, etc.

RUBRICS

The primary way we assess these skills in our STEM-infused classrooms is by using **rubrics**. A rubric is a chart that identifies expected learning outcomes and is used to measure the extent to which a student has met those objectives. This tool greatly decreases subjectivity in grading. For example, a teacher might grade a paper and give one student a B. Twenty papers later, a student who performed similarly on the paper might receive an A or a C if the teacher is grading without any assessment tool. However, if the teacher has a rubric with objectives, he or she has identified exactly what the student must accomplish and how many points the student will receive for the level to which he or she accomplishes that goal. Similarly, in a STEM challenge, a rubric might read, "Student can defend his or her design citing evidence gathered during research." This is, of course, something the teacher would be looking for during grading but would not necessarily show up on a standardized test.

Besides creating an objective way to measure student learning, rubrics also offer the benefit of providing specific feedback to the students. When a student receives a graded rubric, he or she knows exactly how he or she is progressing toward specific learning targets and is able to make adjustments next time. In this way, students assume more ownership of their own learning (see Figure 7.1).

Several times during previous chapters, we looked at Bloom's Taxonomy. But again, when I sit down to write a rubric for a project, I pull that back out. It is very important that our objectives begin with "higher-order" verbs on our rubrics to ensure we are grading rigorous goals for our project. For example, if students were designing a parachute as part of their project, you might be tempted to use an objective such as "Students can identify gravity as the force working against them in this activity." However, this assesses a lower-order skill because the student is essentially just remembering a vocabulary word. On the other hand, you could use this similar but higher-order objective: "Students can defend their design idea by explaining the interaction of forces at work in the challenge." This standard requires students to understand various forces and how they impact one another, apply that content knowledge to the challenge, and provide a defense for their design based on those two things.

Another dynamic I like to add to rubrics sometimes is having students help me identify elements that need to be included on a rubric. Obviously, I have to write the goals in a format that assesses higher-order understanding of content skills, but I often have them help me identify process skills and goals related to their interaction. By doing this, the students take even more ownership of their learning because they feel like they have contributed to the assessment process.

STUDENT GOAL SETTING

Similarly, helping students set goals for themselves is an important part of assessment in the STEM-infused classroom. Many of my colleagues have students identify three to five process-related goals each quarter. The following are examples of goals a student might set:

- I want to do a better job of finding background information to help me come up with a solution to a challenge.
- I want to get along with my teammates better.
- I plan to work on communicating more clearly when I present a project to my classmates.

Physical and Chemical Changes Research

www.padlet.com/wall/hastings_changes

Objective:	Score:	Evidence
Students completed all parts of each task.	1 2 3 4 (5)	
Activate Background Knowledge: Students DESCRIBE both physical and chemical changes accurately.	1 2 3 4 (5)	Team 1 Physical Change- A Physical Change is when you change something but you can put it back together. Chemical Change- A Chemical Change is when something causes a chemical reaction and it doesn't go back to what it used to be. Exactly!
Study Jams: Students DEFEND their answer by APPLYING their understanding of the concepts.	1 2 3 4 (5)	Team 1 Answer- We would rather have a physical change. Reason- If we did a physical change you could still use it because the molecules are still good but in a chemical change the molecules are broken so you can't use it again. Yes! That's a fantastic way to explain it!
Awesome Experiments: Students correctly DIFFERENTIATE between cause and effect in the context of an experiment.	1 2 3 4 (5)	Team 1 Cause- They put the penny in vinegar. Effect- So it rusted.
You Be the Teacher: Students EVALUATE the slide show thoughtfully, including meaningful positive and negative comments.	1 2 (3) 4 5	Team 1 Grade- A- Positive comment- Great explaining Physical changes. Needs improvement- Needs to explain some of the words on chemical change more. Although both of these comments are true, they don't prove to me that you understand the concepts of physical and chemical changes. Remember that each answer you give should be evidence of your understanding and application of these science words.
Let's Focus on Your Brain: Students JUSTIFY their thought process and then DEFEND the correct answer.	1 2 3 4 (5)	Team 1 Missed question- Melting butter for popcorn. Misconception- We thought it was chemical change because it was melted and we thought it couldn't go back to regular. Defense of right answer- It is physical change because if you put the melted butter in a cold place it will harden and go back to regular butter. Even though you missed this question the first time, I can tell you were using what you know about physical and chemical change. Just remember, any change between states (solids, liquids, and gases) is a physical change.
Students used correct capitalization and punctuation on each task.	1 2 3 4 (5)	Nice!
Overall Score:	**33** /35 = **94** %	

SOURCE: Photo by Linda Talley.

- I want to work on listening to my group and thinking about their suggestions instead of thinking in my head about what I am going to say.
- I am going to work on making small, smart adjustments when trying to improve my design.
- I am going to work on asking my group members good questions to start discussions.
- I will work on labeling my blueprints more clearly.
- I am going to do a better job of keeping notes in my improvement log as I work through a challenge.

These goals are often determined based on feedback students have received on rubrics, informal teacher-student interactions, etc. Once per quarter, the teacher may conference with each student in order to discuss his or her progress toward these goals and create new goals.

STUDENT JOURNALING

Another item useful in assessing STEM-infused learning is a STEM journal. This journal is used each time students are working on the design process. In it, the kids write the steps of the engineering design process and keep notes on each step of the process. This often can be used for student reflection as well as evidence for the teacher to grade using a rubric.

IMPROVEMENT LOGS

The students also keep **improvement logs** when doing a design challenge that requires them to make small adjustments many times throughout the project (see Resource H). The improvement log has four columns: (1) Draw your design (or take a picture if you are using a digital version of the improvement log); (2) What happened when you tested? (3) What are you going to do to improve before testing again? (4) What evidence supports the idea that this might work? This helps students to focus on making smart adjustments to their design and defending their adjustments using content knowledge.

TEACHER CLIPBOARD

A teacher clipboard is also a great tool in a STEM-infused classroom. When students are working, the teacher may walk around the classroom, observe, and take notes. Again, this is gathering evidence to help him or her grade each student's rubric at the end of the project. The teacher may be checking off specific objectives on the clipboard or he or she may just take scripted notes.

Another helpful way to use the clipboard is to write quotations you hear students say when they are talking to one another while working. I often write these quotes on the board and use them to spark rich dialogue with the class at the end of the work time. (Sometimes I just carry my phone or an iPad around and dictate these notes in order to record them.)

ASSESSING SOCIAL EMOTIONAL LEARNING

Although this controversial topic has been frequently debated on education blogs and networking groups lately, I do assess social skills in my classroom. I have seen several articles lately debating whether or not social-emotional, or affect, skills should be assessed. As I am sure you know by now, I believe we are charged with developing a whole child into a productive and responsible citizen, and developing his or her ability to collaborate productively is part of that. Therefore, it is important to assess those skills to monitor progress. Those who disagree with my viewpoint on this often say it is not fair to grade students on this because it can be subjective or because it is not a tested, standardized, required skill. My answer to this goes back to what was discussed at the beginning of the chapter—Are we assessing for the sake of recording a number in the gradebook or are we assessing to find areas that need improvement and meeting those needs? If we are looking to improve, then we should be improving the whole child.

STANDARDIZE TESTING AND STEM

Our students are still going to have to take standardized tests. Those are not going away. But in our STEM-infused classrooms, let's reset our focus in assessing back to what it should be—a constant way of monitoring how effectively we are impacting student learning. Dr. Tony Donen, principal of STEM School Chattanooga, in Chattanooga, Tennessee, puts it this way:

> STEM learning is not about students regurgitating information. STEM learning requires students to both acquire knowledge and apply the knowledge with the freedom to fail and opportunity to improve. STEM is about process thinking where students collaborate, critically think, and innovate. When students process well, we win. Show me a student who has learned to collaborate, critically think, and innovate well, and I'll show you a student who is and will be successful. Items such as test scores are not the focus of STEM. Focusing and, more importantly, trusting STEM work is the key piece. Test scores take care of themselves.

Getting everything correct on a multiple choice high stakes state test at the end of the year does not make someone advanced. These questions don't ask us to apply or innovate, they ask us to regurgitate, which is a mediocre skill at best. So . . . getting every mediocre question correct doesn't make someone advanced, it makes them really, really, really mediocre. Requiring someone to find information, pick out what is important, and apply that information to create a new solution is advanced work. STEM implemented well requires students to be advanced thinkers, not really good mediocre thinkers. (personal communication, July 9, 2015)

In other words, assessment in a STEM-infused classroom means setting the bar higher that what is expected on a standardized test. In doing so, the students will learn what they need to know to be successful.

In other words, assessment in a STEM-infused classroom means setting the bar higher that what is expected on a standardized test. In doing so, the students will learn what they need to know to be successful.

Discussion Starters

- What are your beliefs surrounding assessment? How do those beliefs affect your classroom environment?

- What are the advantages and limitations of using rubrics for grading?

- Do your students have individualized goals in your classroom? How might STEM-infusion help you assess individual progress?

- How might an improvement log assist students in building 21st century skills (collaboration, communication, creativity, and critical thinking)?

- Do you believe that social-emotional skills should be assessed? Why or why not?

YOUR NEXT STEP

Print and make copies of the improvement log (Resource H). Implement one of the projects you designed after Chapters 4 to 6. Write a list of academic vocabulary that students should be discussing during the project on the board. Have students document their progress on the improvement log. Ask students to highlight vocabulary on their log.

CHAPTER 8

The Benefits of the STEM Mindset

Risk Taking and Resilience

LOCKED OUT

During my first year teaching in the STEM lab, one of our parent volunteers came in and said, "I have to tell you the story of what happened at our house this past weekend!" She reported that on Friday night her two daughters, who were at the time in first and third grade, had been left home with a babysitter while she and her husband went out. At some point during the evening, the girls and their babysitter went outside to play. When they returned, they found they had accidentally locked the door behind them. They were locked out! The babysitter, who was fairly young and did not have much experience either, began to completely panic. Instead of calmly analyzing the situation, her fear and self-doubt clouded her ability to problem solve.

Those two sweet, STEM-minded girls did not even flinch. Instead, the oldest suggested they pass the ball around between them to calm themselves down a bit. She also proposed each time the ball came to them, they were to brainstorm a solution to the current problem. She explained to her younger sister and babysitter, "It doesn't even have to be a good idea. Just say any idea that comes to your head. Then eventually we can build on each other's thoughts and come up with a doable solution . . . like we do in STEM!" (I am not exaggerating! This is exactly the story as it was told to me.) So the girls began to throw out suggestions:

- "Walk down the road to a neighbor's house and ask to borrow the phone."
- "Search the garage for something to pick the lock."
- "Search the garage for something to slide between the lock and the door."
- "Check each window to see if any are unlocked."
- "Break a window."
- "Make the best of being outside until our parents get back."
- "Look under the mats for hidden keys."

As you can see, none of these suggestions was especially brilliant. It would have made a cool story if the girls had "MacGyvered" some type of amazing invention to jimmy the lock. However, the amazing part of this story is not how they got in. (I actually do not even remember how they ended up solving the problem.) The inspiring part, and the part their mom was so impressed with, is that they were not afraid in the face of a real-world challenge. Instead of panicking in a scary situation, they calmly brainstormed

In short, they had practiced the design process so many times in simulated challenges that it became their go-to approach to solving a problem.

solutions and then patiently tried various ideas until they were able to solve the problem. In short, they had practiced the design process so many times in simulated challenges that it became their go-to approach to solving a problem.

A MINDSET SHIFT

In the traditional classroom, students generally focus on giving the right answer. They solve a math problem and get credit for the correct solution. They write an essay and receive red marks for using poor conventions. Everything is black and white, right or wrong. Trends in education, such as constructed response assessments, call for a more process-focused learning experience. However, students often feel very uncomfortable with the idea of productive struggle.

Practicing STEM in the elementary classroom gives students a framework for working through the unknown and a safety net for risk-taking. For example, in one activity, students were challenged to design storm shelters that would hold up to wind and water weathering (see Resource I). However, before they could design their shelter, they had to create their own recipe for clay using flour, salt, oil, and warm water. Students also had to budget money to purchase their materials. At first, most groups created clay that was either extremely dry or extremely wet. They had to gradually adjust their recipe until they found the perfect consistency.

Although improving a recipe is a very nonthreatening situation, we found that, over time, this ability to try something without knowing the outcome carried over into all situations. When a student did not know how to solve a math problem, instead of shutting down, he or she started brainstorming ways to approach it. Instead of feeling like a failure when he or she arrived at a wrong answer, the student viewed it as an opportunity to *improve* his or her thought process.

In learning this, students also discovered that self-reflection is part of growth. On many challenges, the students and I work together to identify academic and performance standards for each challenge and create rubrics to measure progress toward these goals. On others, the students use a simple T-chart labeled "What happened when you tested?" on one side and "What are you going to change in order to improve? Why?" on the other. In using these, the students learn to reflect on their own misunderstandings or mistakes and use those to improve. They are learning to embrace productive struggle.

GROWTH VERSUS FIXED MINDSETS

This belief in oneself to overcome difficult tasks is evidence of what Carol Dweck refers to as a **growth mindset** (Dweck, 2010). Some educators argue that student attitudes such as grit, or resilience, are static or at least outside of the school's control. This, on the other hand, is evidence of a fixed mindset. A fixed mindset is based on the belief that intelligence is largely outside of one's control—some are born smart and some are not. But a growth mindset asserts that anyone can grow through effective instruction and effort.

So it is essential that we as teachers project this message that intelligence is something attainable for anyone who is willing to work hard. Then we have to support kids in struggling through hard challenges, helping them learn from their mistakes, and eventually gain confidence in their own ability to attack a problem.

According to Dweck's research, a student who has a growth mindset is more motivated, which eventually results in higher academic success. It makes sense, doesn't it? If a kid thinks there is nothing he or she can do to get smart, then why try? So it is essential that we as teachers project this message that intelligence is something attainable for anyone who is willing to work hard. Then we have to support kids in struggling through hard challenges, helping them learn from their mistakes, and eventually gain confidence in their own ability to attack a problem.

GROWING FROM STEM

When I taught fourth grade, I distinctly remember one little girl coming in on the first day of school and saying, "I'm just not good at math. My mom says she wasn't either so she says she understands that I can't do it." This was my stream of consciousness at that moment: "What??? How is it that a kid who is only nine years old has already decided she isn't going to be successful in math for the rest of her life? And who does this mom think she is telling this baby that she's not smart? And what in the world am I supposed to do to teach a kid who already believes she's unteachable? And what can I say in this very moment to start building her confidence and fighting this uphill battle?"

And so I took a deep breath and told that sweet girl, "By the end of the year, you are going to be able to say you are a math genius and mean it." Before I could teach her the very first math skill, I had to convince her she was capable of learning that skill.

From that point on, I thought a lot about how to convince students that failure leads to success. The engineering design process teaches just that. Through STEM-infusion, students learn that messing up just gives you a little more data to make adjustments. They learn that smart adjustments lead to success. And they carry this lesson on to all of the curriculum.

STUDENT EMPOWERMENT

As my colleagues in the school district have discussed transforming our learning environments into 21st century classrooms this year, we have had some

Figure 8.1 Student Empowerment Matrix

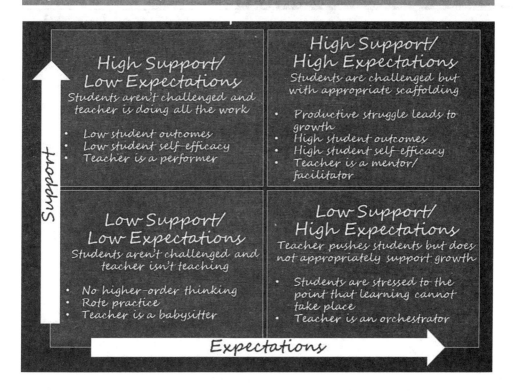

interesting discussions on the balance between support and expectations. I created the graphic in Figure 8.1 to show this idea.

It was interesting to hear teachers reflect on their own teaching in relationship to this matrix. Many of the elementary teachers admitted they erred on the side of over-supporting. We have a hard time letting those little ones struggle. But struggle is an opportunity for growth when it is accompanied by appropriate facilitation and

It is important to constantly self-assess to make sure we are maximizing student growth as we both challenge and support them.

support by the teacher. I include this graphic as a self-reflection tool for teachers who are implementing STEM-infusion. It is important to constantly self-assess to make sure we are maximizing student growth as we both challenge and support them.

Discussion Starters

- How do students in your classroom currently approach difficult situations or react to perceived failure?

- Do you have a growth mindset? In what ways do you show your students that you believe in their ability to change, grow, and improve?

- What other factors must accompany struggle in order for it to be productive instead of discouraging?

- Describe an example of a lesson in which your students had to systematically work through a difficult challenge. How did you support that struggle?

YOUR NEXT STEP

Place yourself on the following scale for each question.

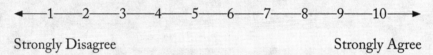

Strongly Disagree   Strongly Agree

1. Every student in my class can learn.
2. I can impact my students' basic level of intelligence.
3. My students believe in their own ability to grow.
4. My students are willing to take risks.
5. My students believe that failure leads to success.
6. My students strategically attack problems they are not sure how to solve.
7. I provide opportunities for students to improve when they are not successful the first time.
8. I acknowledge my students' effort, not just their successes.
9. Growth (as opposed to proficiency) is the goal in my classroom.
10. I provide my students opportunities to reflect on their progress.

Each of these statements reflects a growth mindset. If your answers tended to lean more toward a fixed mindset, invite a colleague to help you brainstorm changes that would make your classroom more growth centered.

CHAPTER 9

Student Collaboration

LEGO TRENCH

Imagine this. . . . You walk into a classroom and all the student chairs and desks are stacked in a corner. A trench made of thousands of Legos (see Figure 9.1) is poured down the center of the room (see Resource J). On the board you see one word—TRUCK. The students are sitting on the floor along both sides of the Lego trench, facing a partner across the trench from them. And behind each line of students sits a file folder standing up on end hiding a picture of a truck. You notice, however, that the pictures are different—one shows a small red pickup truck while the other shows a massive, red 18-wheeler. The students are enthusiastically bellowing to their partners' statements such as, "A red truck! With silver on it? Yeah, that's what I saw too." What is going on here? And how could this possibly be a worthwhile use of time in a classroom? Unless, maybe it is recess.

Except it is not recess. This is an exercise in communication. One of our primary goals for the STEM lab when we started planning in the first year was that it would be a place where students very intentionally practiced the collaborative skills they would need to interact with others in school and in a 21st century

Figure 9.1 Students practice thorough and deliberate communication skills using the Lego trench activity.

SOURCE: Photo by Linda Talley.

STEM-INFUSING THE ELEMENTARY CLASSROOM

workforce. The very first lessons I ever planned were group challenges in which students had to share responsibility in every step of the engineering design process. However, one thing I did not consider early on is that collaborative skills are not intuitive for elementary school students. They are still very "me-centric," and most do not have the maturity to consider the good of the team above their own point of view.

In the classroom described above, students were doing an activity to help them practice communicating differing ideas clearly. The instructions were the following:

- I revealed a word on the board. The students were told they would have to build a model of that object with their partner across the trench using Legos.

- The students on each side of the trench went and looked at a picture of that word behind the file folder.

- The students were to come back to their partner and explain what they saw in the picture before they began building a model together. (The trick was at first the students did not know they were looking at two different pictures. They assumed their partner had the same picture in their heads as they had in their own.)

- After they had explained the picture, they built a model that compromised the ideas and input of both students.

This activity worked really well for practicing communication because it simulated what really happens when students try to build together in a design challenge. All students involved have their own mental image of what the finished product should look like. They also usually assume the image they have in their head is the same image their group members have also. Then when a group member does something that demonstrates the incongruence, the child gets frustrated that he or she is "changing the plan." In actuality, the group members just did not communicate thoroughly in the first place.

In the Lego trench activity, I planted conflicting mental interpretations of the word on the board in their brain by showing partners' different pictures. They were then forced to communicate with each other to understand the picture in the other person's mind. From there, they could work to compromise and combine the two pictures into a Lego structure.

FOUNDATION OF COMMUNICATION

My purpose in telling you all this is to say that communication and collaboration skills can and need to be explicitly taught and practiced in the elementary classroom. The following are helpful lessons I have learned about teaching kids to work together:

- It will be hard at first. At the beginning of the school year, you are probably going to think "my kids just can't handle group work." I hear that all the time. And it is true—I have yet to see a class that started the year already knowing how to work well with each other. However, practice makes perfect. The more students practice collaboration, the smoother it gets. And the smoother it gets, the less students will have to focus on their interpersonal skills. And the less they have to focus on their interpersonal skills, the more you will see the benefits of synergy within student groups.

- Taking time to practice these skills early on will save you time later. This is a trick all teachers learn early in their career. If you spend the first few days of school establishing clear procedures (i.e., for lining up, turning in homework, morning routine, transitions), you will spend much less time dealing with issues throughout the year because most students know what is expected. We have learned the best defense is a good offense. The same goes for teaching collaborative skills. The Lego activity described before would not be difficult to tie to a Common Core standard for language arts or math. It might look like chaos to anyone who walks into the classroom after instructions were given. However, teaching kids to be aware of other people's mental images, allowing them to practice communicating those images, and facilitating discussion on how to compromise those images are essential procedures to establish early in a STEM-infused elementary classroom. Otherwise, you will spend all year putting out fires between students who cannot agree on a design idea.

- Create an anchor chart with sentence starters for communication, and refer to it often. In my classroom, I have a poster (see Figure 9.2).

Early in the year, my assistant and I role-played a conversation in which we used these sentence starters to resolve a misunderstanding. We walked individual groups through using these sentence starters to more clearly communicate with each other during group activities. We challenged them to consider how they could affirm ideas they liked instead of only focusing on those they did not like. We taught them that disagreeing was normal and acceptable as long as it was handled and resolved respectfully. And these simple sentence starters became part of natural speech within the classroom (see Figure 9.2).

As a class, determine a set of norms for how different issues will be handled.

- Teach kids to do a brain check. When groups are discussing ideas, call a timeout right in the middle of their discussion. Have them think

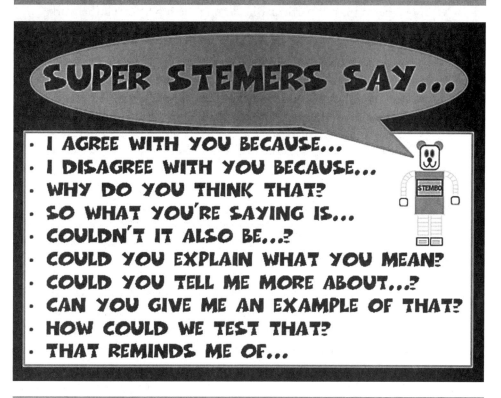

SOURCE: Created by Linda Talley.

about what they were just thinking of. Ask them, "If you were not the one talking when I called 'brain check,' what were you thinking about? Were you really listening to the person who was talking in your group? Or were you thinking about your own ideas and planning what you were going to say next? How would you feel if the next time it is your turn to talk, your teammates were not actively listening?" Again, this little interruption is so worthwhile. It is a metacognitive practice that will serve them well in any relationship.

- Put the students in charge of accountability and conflict resolution. As a class, determine a set of norms for how different issues will be handled. For example:
  - When disagreement arises in a small group, will we make a decision by majority rules? Or will we take turns getting to make decisions? Or will we pick a number, flip a coin, or pull a name out of a hat and let that person decide?
  - If someone is dominating the group, how can the other students address him or her to restore balance? Do they need to tell a teacher?

Or can they speak freely about it because they have already agreed at the onset that they want everyone to participate equally?

  o If one person is not participating, letting the others do all the work, how will the group respond? Will the group assign him or her a task? Does one person need to pull him or her aside and have a private conversation with him or her?

- Once the students are consistently communicating and collaborating using these norms, you can begin to introduce leadership skills as well. Each day, designate a group leader to facilitate their group. Discuss with the students that the job of a leader is not to boss people around but to bring out the best in the people he or she is leading. Have the leader practice being a good listener and making decisions that benefit the entire team. Also, discuss how to be a good follower. This accomplishes two purposes: preparing the students with an additional important life skill and ensuring that designs are powered by student brainpower (not the teacher's).

  All of these are examples of situations that will arise at some point. If a group has agreed upon a course of action before the conflict arises, students are more likely to be able to resolve the conflict themselves instead of needing an adult to solve it for them. (Of course, the teacher will need to walk them through this resolution more often at first until the students learn to do it more independently.)

- Teamwork directly correlates to success in a challenge. I wish so badly that three years ago I had started documenting all of the times this was true. In fact, if you are just starting STEM-infusion for the first time in your classroom, I would recommend hanging up a tally sheet somewhere in the room and recording the number of times this correlation occurs in your classroom from now on. If a group gets along well and every member is focusing on the goal of the challenge instead of getting his or her own way, the team very often successfully designs a viable solution to the challenge. On the other hand, if a group argues, they almost always either do not complete the challenge or their design is not successful. Seriously, document it and see.

- Communication and collaboration become part of your culture—extending to all parts of the day. When students practice these skills in a STEM-infused classroom, they use them not just for STEM challenges but also all day long. They get along better on the playground. Reading groups run smoother. It is even easier to make a seating chart because there are not as many students who would need an island for themselves to keep from getting in fights with others.

RICHNESS OF THE INTERACTION

This week, I was working with a third-grade class, reading a text about how technology has changed sports. The teacher and I have co-taught STEM-infused lessons weekly since the beginning of school. In the beginning, the communication was surface level, and I sometimes wondered if the learning objective was being met in a sufficiently rigorous way. However, this week, the students were reflecting on two STEM challenges they had done in relationship to the sports technology story (see Resources K and L). In one challenge, they had redesigned a tennis shoe for their teacher to wear while running. In another, they had redesigned a football helmet, which they tested on a water balloon "brain."

As I listened to the students talk, they compared and contrasted the two projects. They identified that in the first project, they had focused more on the comfort of the tennis shoe. On the second, their highest priority had been safety. They then pondered how the shoe would be different if safety had been a higher priority and how the helmet would have changed if comfort had been the focus. What really impressed me was when one student brought up the question of whether those priorities were defined by the teacher in the constraints of the challenge or whether the group had self-imposed them. These are third graders having a fairly philosophical conversation about priorities and influence and motivation! That is higher-order thinking! And we could not have gotten there if STEM had not been the language of the classroom all year long. In fact, I did the same project with another class who had not been doing STEM all year and only heard very surface-level discussion. In the second class, the kids really had to spend a lot of time resolving disagreements and figuring out who would do what. When communication and collaboration are explicitly and continuously taught and practiced, those issues get out of the way and the deep, insightful discussions can prevail.

> *When communication and collaboration are explicitly and continuously taught and practiced, those issues get out of the way and the deep, insightful discussions can prevail.*

- What types of frustrations have you experienced when it comes to student communication? What misconceptions did your students hold in that situation?

- Share procedures that you establish in your classroom that build student communication skills.

- How can you help your students move from just getting along during group work to facilitating their own higher-order conversations?

- How do the communication skills practiced in a STEM-infused classroom help students prepare for their future?

YOUR NEXT STEP

Give your class the opportunity to develop a set of norms for group work, including the following: a conflict resolution plan, ways to engage students who are not participating, and ways to deal with students who are dominating the group.

CHAPTER 10

Leadership for Change

A REALLY HARD NIGHT

At the beginning of the year, our district put on a community event in which families of students could come and hear the vision of our district for 21st century learning and technology integration. During one part of the night, one of my colleagues and I were designated to demonstrate an elementary lesson plan. We created an excellent first-grade lesson that integrated research, iPads, STEM, and other important 21st century skills. It was set to be quite an exciting presentation.

However, the night of the event, we stood in front of a packed auditorium and our technology malfunctioned. We had planned to reflect our iPad onto the projector but it would not reflect. Although we explained our lesson without the visuals, it was quite embarrassing to stand before all of those people to demonstrate technology integration with a technology glitch. It did not help when I sat down and realized my pants had been unzipped the whole time.

The whole experience was so far from what we expected it to be that it was easy to laugh about it afterward. Parents good-naturedly complemented our poise in handling the situation and said the vision was still portrayed without the help of the visuals. In fact, the banter that took place because of this glitch ended up helping our purpose: to build relationships between our schools and the people we serve. As we draw near to the end of the book, I want to address one more topic that has been crucial to the success of STEM-integration in our schools—leading change through relationships.

PROGRESS AS AN EXPECTATION

By now, you have seen evidence of the dramatic instructional shift that has taken place in our school toward STEM-infusing our elementary classrooms. I will not pretend we have arrived at some extraordinary final goal, that we have it all figured out, or that our staff is completely comfortable with this drastic, pedagogical change. However, in this now three-year-old process, we are further along in the transition than we expected to be. In fact, I can confidently say that every teacher has moved in this direction, whether by leaps and bounds or by cautious baby steps, and we have been careful to maintain progress as our only expectation.

That in itself has been a major contributing factor to the success of this change process. We were clear on the fact that we would not be setting sweeping standards and timelines for every teacher. Instead, we helped each teacher identify his or her next step and supported him or her in taking it. In doing this, our highly enthusiastic risk-takers could take off and explore new ways of doing things, while our more cautious teachers could take calculated steps forward.

I feel I should stop right here to clarify something. Both of these groups of people are essential to the change process: Those who take off pave the way to try new things and those who take cautious steps forward help refine the process. If you are in the latter group—you have read this book somewhat nervously, believing in the need for change but not sure you can see yourself jumping in head first—you are crucial to the change in your school. You are the ones who refine processes and perfect details along the way. Just keep taking the next step forward. Keep trying to perfect one thing before moving to the next. And if you, like me, are in the former group, keep dreaming big and taking risks in trying out new things. But both groups—listen to each other. That will be the key to balancing this initiative. That will be what sustains this change over time.

> *Those who take off pave the way to try new things and those who take cautious steps forward help refine the process.*

In doing this, we have found that our teachers have not only discovered the value of STEM-integration but also implemented it willingly. Because of that, I've frequently been asked this question: How do you get teacher buy-in? In this final chapter, I will share several factors that I believe played a role in developing a culture of acceptance for STEM-infusing the elementary classroom.

MODELING

In our school system, the concept of STEM was first introduced by adding a STEM lab to each school. At the elementary level, the students attended STEM once a week as part of their special areas schedule. As the STEM teacher, I planned and implemented cross-curricular STEM lessons, giving students a baseline understanding of the STEM concepts, as well as the impact STEM could have on their futures. Students who were quickly engaged by the interactive lessons embraced STEM immediately. As students began to excitedly share what they were doing in STEM class with their homeroom teachers, it opened the door for conversations among the faculty. In this regard, the fact that our district administration believed in the importance of STEM enough to fund a position for a STEM teacher was the first step in getting our teachers to buy in. The teachers felt they had the resources and support from the administration, instead of a mandated program.

PARENT INVOLVEMENT

In the very early days of our STEM class, it occurred to us that parent involvement would be our most precious resource. Therefore, we compiled an email contact list of all parents who were willing to volunteer in STEM class or help us gather resources for the STEM lab. We also created a blog where we posted pictures of students doing their STEM projects. As a result of these two forms of communication with parents, we had dozens of parents volunteering regularly, we collected an abundance of materials (everything from cardboard tubes to Legos), and our parent-teacher organization even raised enough money to purchase 10 iPads for the STEM lab. Just by publicizing what we were doing and bringing parents on board, a tone of appreciation and support for STEM became a part of our school's culture.

GOAL SETTING

At the beginning of our second year of having a STEM class in the school, a colleague and I introduced the concept of STEM-integration to the faculty. We had learned about a high school where students were presented with a challenge or scenario at the beginning of a semester and all content area teachers helped students gain pieces of information needed to design a solution throughout the term. We felt this same concept could be applied at the elementary level but within a shorter time frame. After casting a vision for STEM-infusion, highlighting the need to teach 21st century skills and providing sample STEM-infused lessons, each teacher set a goal for the year. Some wanted to observe STEM-integration in other classrooms, others agreed to try a project or two, while still others planned to implement STEM-infusion on a regular basis. Again, the expectation was not that the teachers met a minimum requirement but that they would take steps toward moving in that direction. Consequently, most were further along in the process at the end of the year than they originally intended to be.

In our third year, I became a full-time instructional coach, specifically to support STEM and technology integration (as we were beginning our 1:1 iPad initiative as well). One way I helped teachers set goals was by developing a **teacher IEP**— "Individual Exploration Plan." At the beginning of the year, I sat down for just a few minutes with each teacher, and we set individualized goals for the year. The teacher then identified what his or her next steps would be and what support he or she would need in order to get there (help planning, co-teaching, finding resources, etc.). Throughout the year, I have been able to sit down with a number of teachers to update this document and look at ways to continue moving forward.

SHARING RESOURCES AND PROVIDING SUPPORT

At this point in the transition, the STEM classroom became a resource for teachers. They came to borrow materials, to brainstorm ideas, to plan lessons, etc. In one particularly exciting incident, a teacher who was very concerned about transforming her instruction came to me for help. We sat down together and looked at the material she would be teaching and began to co-plan a unit using the conceptual approach. I spent short blocks of time over the next couple of days in her classroom, sometimes teaching while she observed, and other times supporting her while she taught. The very next week, I walked into her classroom to find her students participating in a new STEM-infused lesson she had designed. With a little bit of scaffolding, she developed the confidence to step outside of the way she had always taught.

TEACHING TEAMS

As the STEM-infusion started catching on with a few teachers in our building, they began to spread the word to their teammates and inviting them to participate in planning for STEM-infused activities (see Figure 10.1). One team in particular was an amazing model of collaborative planning. Each week, team members set aside one afternoon to come together and look at their curriculum for the following week. One person would throw out an idea and the others would build on it. Within 30 or 45 minutes, they would have a week-long STEM challenge planned together. This year, they have continued to tweak and perfect those challenges. But an "all in" attitude from the team was the key to the growth of STEM-infusion for that group of teachers.

TEACHER TRUST AND AUTONOMY

This last element that continues to foster teacher buy-in with STEM-infusion brings us back to the focus on relationships we started with at the beginning of this

Figure 10.1 Teacher collaboration is an essential component of STEM-infusion.

SOURCE: Photo by Linda Talley.

chapter. Our school administrators trust in the professional skills of the teachers. They give us the freedom to make instructional decisions based on the individual needs of our students. They lead us by complimenting our strengths and making helpful suggestions to improve our weaknesses. Because of that, we have not felt pressure to make sweeping changes all at once. Instead, we have felt supported as we have tweaked and tested STEM-infusion. This atmosphere of trust and autonomy is a prerequisite for positive change.

CLOSING

Perhaps these factors contributing to the success we have had so far with teacher buy-in are not all together unique to STEM-integration. Many of them would work for any school transition that requires a mindset shift for all stakeholders (see Figure 10.2).

Figure 10.2 Learners in our school have benefitted greatly from the student-focused attitudes of teachers who are embracing pedagogical change.

SOURCE: Photo by Linda Talley.

As far as we have come, we have forever to go. This process is part of a limitless transition toward more student-centered, thought-inspiring, and challenge-based learning opportunities for our students.

As you begin the process of STEM-infusing your classroom, school, and district, I want to leave you with three additional resources to help in the planning process: two different templates for STEM-infusion lesson plans (Resources M and N) and a list of additional ideas for STEM-infusion activities (Resource O). Happy STEM-infusing!

> As far as we have come, we have forever to go. This process is part of a limitless transition toward more student-centered, thought-inspiring, and challenge-based learning opportunities for our students.

- When it comes to pedagogical change, are you the type of teacher who takes "leaps and bounds" or one who takes "cautious baby steps"? In either case, what will your next step look like as you integrate what you have learned in this book?

- What role will you play in the change process in your school?

- How will you communicate your vision for STEM-infusion to parents?

- In what ways do you feel empowered by your administration to make instructional changes? If it is going to take some convincing, what evidence from this book could you use to justify the change?

YOUR NEXT STEP

Recruit teachers within your school to plan STEM-infused activities with. Set goals for how often you plan to do these activities, how often you will meet, and how you will share what you are doing with other teachers within your school.

Resource A

Pipeline Lesson Plan

STEM-Infused Lesson Plan Example

Title: Pipeline Challenge (Chapter 1)

Recommended Grade Levels: 3–5

Academic Concepts:

- **Language Arts.** Cause and effect, *Alaskan Pipeline* basal story, research skills, defending an opinion with evidence
  - CCSS.ELA-LITERACY.RI.3.1. Ask and answer questions to demonstrate understanding of a text, referring explicitly to the text as the basis for the answers.
  - CCSS.ELA-LITERACY.RI.3.3. Describe the relationship between a series of historical events, scientific ideas or concepts, or steps in technical procedures in a text using language that pertains to time, sequence, and cause and effect.

- **Math.** Triangles
  - CCSS.MATH.CONTENT.3.G.A.1. Understand that shapes in different categories (e.g., rhombuses, rectangles, and others) may share attributes (e.g., having four sides) and that the shared attributes can define a larger category (e.g., quadrilaterals). Recognize rhombuses, rectangles, and squares as examples of quadrilaterals, and draw examples of quadrilaterals that do not belong to any of these subcategories.

- **Science.** Environmental effects, renewable and nonrenewable resources
  - NGSS 3-LS4-4. Make a claim about the merit of a solution to a problem caused when the environment changes and the types of plants and animals that live there may change.

- **Social Studies.** Branches of government, checks and balances
  - NSS-C.K-4.1. What is government?

(Continued)

(Continued)

Essential Question:

Should the Keystone Pipeline be allowed?

Design Challenge:

Build a pipeline that allows 200 milliliters of water to run a distance of 1 meter from one cup to another.

Supplies:

- Craft sticks
- Cardboard tubes
- Straws
- Foam cups
- Paper
- Classroom chairs may be used to elevate
- Tape
- 200-ml beaker of water
- Meter stick

Steps:

- Students do background research to understand the branches of government, the process of a bill becoming a law, and the system of checks and balances. Teacher provides videos, articles, and discussion questions through Blackboard, Padlet, QR codes, or school website.

- Present students with an article about the Keystone bill. (The article should be balanced in its political views and describe the supporter's viewpoints on increasing jobs and financial benefits and the opposition's stance on environmental impacts.)

- Show students a map of the proposed Keystone pipeline and the existing one. Since the two form a triangle, the students can use their geometry skills to determine the difference in distance oil would travel in the two pipelines.

- Encourage the students to look at a historical perspective to create a list of pros and cons for the pipeline. (Scott Foresman has a fourth-grade reading basal that includes a leveled reader on the Alaskan Pipeline.) The students use this reader to develop a pros and cons graphic.

- Have students "put themselves on a line." The students have a pipeline labeled 1–10: 1 being completely for the pipeline and 10 being completely against it. They decided where they would rank their opinions at that point.

- Partner students with someone who believes very differently than they do.

- The students' design challenge is to build a pipeline that allows 200 ml of water to run a distance of 1 meter from one cup to another. (The really interesting and beneficial part of this challenge is the conversation between the two students who have very different concerns for their pipeline. The "big oil" student is worried about profit loss if the pipeline leaks, while the "environmentalist" worries about the effects of an oil spill.)

Assessment:

- Students participate in a mock debate where each student is responsible for a 1-minute argument, either pro or con.

- Teacher will evaluate speeches using a rubric.

- Depending on grade level and individual students, you may differentiate by having grade-level and below students write "opening arguments" while the students who need more of a challenge prepare to respond with "rebuttals."

Resource B

Volcano Lesson Plan

Title: Volcano Challenge (Chapter 3)
Recommended Grade Levels: 1–3

Academic Concepts:
 	
• **Language Arts.** Compare and contrast Language Experience Approach (LEA) to writing
   ○ CCSS.ELA-LITERACY.RI.1.3. Describe the connection between two individuals, events, ideas, or pieces of information in a text.
 	
• **Science.** Landforms, volcanos, chemical reactions
   ○ 4-ESS1-1. Identify evidence from patterns in rock formations and fossils in rock layers to support an explanation for changes in a landscape over time.

Essential Question: How is a model volcano like and unlike a real volcano? Is the model an accurate portrayal of volcanos?
Design Challenge: Create an infographic comparing and contrasting a model volcano with a real volcano.
Supplies: • Plastic bottle • Vinegar • Baking soda

- Dish soap
- Red food coloring
- Covering for volcano (can do papier-mâché or salt dough but a paper bag upside down with a hole in it works too)
- iPads with Volcano 360 app OR video of volcano erupting
- iPads with Popplet app, Inspiration Maps app, or other digital idea mapping software (or just paper and markers)

Steps:

- Explain the steps of the LEA process to students (shared experience, creating a text, read and revise, read and reread, extension activity) and that you will be doing two different LEAs and then comparing.
- Begin by doing the volcano demonstration.
- Next, the students narrate a summary of the experience in whole-group as the teacher transcribes it on the board to create a text.
- Teacher leads students in editing and revising the text to improve the writing.
- Students practice reading the text together chorally, echo, partner read, etc.
- After that, have students participate in a virtual volcano tour on the Volcano 360 app. (The app allows students to navigate a 360-degree helicopter view over an erupting volcano and take pictures.)
- Repeat the LEA process with this activity. (With older students, you may want to have them do this writing independently, modeled after the previous one.)
- Break students up into teams of two or three. Challenge each team to create an infographic comparing and contrasting the two experiences.

Assessment:

- Students present their infographic to the class.
- They then explain and defend their answer to the essential question— Is the model an accurate portrayal of volcanos?
- Remember that we are looking for unpredictable outcomes when we create relevant activities. Therefore, all infographics will turn out differently. They may also answer the essential question differently, and if they defend it with appropriate evidence, it could be answered either way.

(Continued)

(Continued)

- Teacher assesses using a rubric.
- Teacher may choose to extend this by allowing the students to publish their infographics online.

Resource C

Candy Cane Lesson Plan

Title: Candy Cane Challenge (Chapter 3)
Recommended Grade Levels: 3–5

Academic Concepts:
 	
 • **Language Arts.** Making inferences, defending with evidence, persuasive writing
    ○ CCSS.ELA-LITERACY.RI.4.1. Refer to details and examples in a text when explaining what the text says explicitly and when drawing inferences from the text.
 	
 • **Science.** Environmental effects
    ○ 3-LS4-4. Make a claim about the merit of a solution to a problem caused when the environment changes and the types of plants and animals that live there may change.
 	
 • **Math.** Addition and subtraction with money, multiplication, division
    ○ CCSS.MATH.CONTENT.4.NBT.B.4. Fluently add and subtract multi-digit whole numbers using the standard algorithm.
 	
 • **Social Studies.** Economic impact
    ○ NSS-EC.K-4.5. Gain from trade.

Essential Question: What factors must a company consider in order to increase profit on a good?
Design Challenge: You are a packaging engineer in charge of designing a new package for shipping candy canes.   *(Continued)*

(Continued)

Supplies:

- Candy canes
- Plastic wrap
- Cotton balls
- Construction paper
- Shoeboxes
- Rubber bands
- Tape
- Craft sticks

Steps:

- Students read an article on how candy canes are made. They then discussed in their project groups (or 3–4 students) how that information might impact their design.

- Next, students watched a *Design Squad Nation* video clip on packaging engineers. They then brainstormed a list of factors they would need to consider in their packaging design (safety of the environment, cost of production, appeal to buyers, protection of product in packaging, etc.).

- The students then "purchased" their materials. The teacher prices all of the supplies, and students had to keep a tab of materials purchased in order to later calculate their price per unit.

- The students then drew and labeled a blueprint of their packaging (on Engineering Design Log).

- Next the students had to figure out the cost per unit of their candy cane package.
  - Cost for candy canes = Number of candy canes that fit in package × 2 cents per candy cane
  - Cost of packaging materials = Sum of all supplies
  - Total cost for box of candy canes = Cost of candy canes + cost of packaging
  - Cost per unit = Total cost of box of candy canes ÷ number of candy canes per box

- Depending on grade level, you may need to lead them through this process or let them try to work it out for themselves.

- Groups ordered their cost per unit with other groups in order to find out which group would be offering the best bargain.

- Groups of students then built their candy cane packaging.

- To test the packages, we simulated "shipping and handling" by passing the candy cane packages around the room, dropping them, stacking them, etc.

- Students reflected on what they would do differently if they had a chance to improve their design (on Engineering Design Log).

Assessment:

- Students created a sales pitch to convince the president of the candy cane company that their design would be best.
- The students had a choice of using three different apps that we had used previously and that they were able to use independently:
  - Adobe Voice
  - iMovie
  - Green Screen
- Teacher assessed the sales pitches using a rubric.

Resource D

Germs Lesson Plan

STEM-Infused Lesson Plan Example

Title: Germs Challenge (Chapter 4)
Recommended Grade Levels: K–1

Academic Concepts:
 	
    • **Language Arts.** Drawing conclusions, character interactions
        ○ CCSS.ELA-LITERACY.RL.K.3. With prompting and support, identify characters, settings, and major events in a story.
 	
    • **Math.** Fact families, graphing
        ○ CCSS.MATH.CONTENT.K.OA.A.3. Decompose numbers less than or equal to 10 into pairs in more than one way, e.g., by using objects or drawings, and record each decomposition by a drawing or equation.
 	
    • **Science.** Health and wellness, scientific method
        ○ K-2-ETS1-1. Ask questions, make observations, and gather information about a situation people want to change to define a simple problem that can be solved through the development of a new or improved object or tool.
 	
    • **Social Studies.** Community
        ○ NSS-C.K-4.5. Roles of the citizen.

Essential Question: How can we prevent illness in our classroom?
Design Challenge: One student comes to school sick. What might happen to the class by the end of the day? Why would that happen? With your group, design a solution to keep it from happening.

Supplies:

- Poster board
- Markers
- Hand sanitizer
- Wipes
- Soap
- Other materials per student request if available

Steps:

- Begin by discussing the questions in the design challenge:
  - If one student comes to school sick, what might happen by the end of the day?
  - Why might that happen?

- Break students into groups and ask each student to discuss this question:
  - What could we do to try to prevent that from happening?

- After students have had a chance to initially discuss a plan, lead them in connecting their plan to the concept of cause and effect.
  - What is the cause of students getting sick?
  - What effect do we hope to have when we create and implement our plan?

- Next, help the students link cause and effect across disciplines by creating math tasks that relate to our illness scenario:
  - Twenty kids came to school, but three of them went home sick. How many students were still at school? (Seventeen.)
  - What was the effect of three kids going home? (There were fewer students in the class.)

- Then give students time to design a plan to reduce the spread of germs in the classroom.

- Begin a line graph of the number of kids absent every day beginning 10 days before implementing the class's plan.

- Continue tracking the number of students absent during calendar time each day for the next 10 days.

(Continued)

(Continued)

Assessment:

- Teacher can assess math tasks throughout the week.
- Student can assess student understanding of cause and effect by taking anecdotal notes on a clipboard during large group discussions and small group planning sessions.
- After the data has been tracked for 10 days, the teacher may give students a chance to communicate the results of their intervention with other students in the school by creating a public service announcement, posters, etc.

Resource E

Top Secret Message Lesson Plan

STEM-Infused Lesson Plan Example

Title: Top Secret Message Challenge (Chapter 5)
Recommended Grade Levels: 2–4

Academic Concepts:
 	
• **Language Arts.** Author's purpose, persuasive writing
   ○ CCSS.ELA-LITERACY.W.4.1. Write opinion pieces on topics or texts, supporting a point of view with reasons and information.
 	
• **Math.** Fractions
   ○ CCSS.MATH.CONTENT.4.NF.B.3.D. Solve word problems involving addition and subtraction of fractions referring to the same whole and having like denominators, e.g., by using visual fraction models and equations to represent the problem.
 	
• **Science.** Forces and motion vocabulary (gravity, inertia, point of reference, speed, force, friction)
   ○ 3-PS2-1. Plan and conduct an investigation to provide evidence of the effects of balanced and unbalanced forces on the motion of an object.

Essential Question: What forces must we overcome to get the top secret message to the prince or princess (teacher) in the tower?
Design Challenge: Design something that will allow you to safely send a top secret message to the prince or princess in the tower. (The tower is 10 feet away and 6 feet in the air with a moat in between.) *(Continued)*

(Continued)

Supplies:

- 12 pieces of paper
- 8 paper clips
- 15 rubber bands
- 3 feet of masking tape
- 20 feet of yarn
- 1 improvement log

(This is a limited materials challenge. Once the materials have been used up, the students must creatively rearrange them to continue improving.)

Steps:

- Teach a regular writing lesson as you always would. Tell the students, however, that you are not going to turn in the assignment in the conventional way. Instead, your assignment has become a top secret message that must be relayed to the prince or princess (teacher) stuck in the tower of a castle.
- The teacher presents the challenge and materials to the students.
- Students do Ask, Imagine, and Plan steps on their Engineering Design Log.
- Groups of students begin building a prototype to get their secret message to the prince or princess in the tower. (Ideas kids have come up with in the past include paper airplanes, zip lines, pulleys, fishing poles, etc. However, it is best not to give them any suggestions at first and let them be creative.)
- Each time a group tests their prototype, they must fill out the improvement log to record what happened when they tested, what they are going to do differently the next time, and why. (This is where that science vocabulary needs to show up in order to show that the students understand the concepts.)
- On this challenge, they will also record what fraction (in lowest terms) of their materials they have used up at that point.
- As groups test, the teacher gives feedback about the prototype. For example, the student attaches his or her secret message to a paper airplane and then throws it across the moat:
  - If it does not make it and it lands in the moat, make the students create something they can use to retrieve it out of their materials. (Don't let them get in the moat to get it.)

- If it makes it to the prince or princess, ask them how they could make the trip "safer" for the message in order to improve.

- Even if an attempt is successful, have students continue to improve and come up with better solutions until time is called.

Assessment:

- The student turns in his or her writing assignment (which will be assessed by the rubric for language arts).

- The student also turns in the improvement log (which is assessed for understanding of science concepts as well as fractions in lowest terms).

Resource F

Baseball Lesson Plan

STEM-Infused Lesson Plan Example

Title: Baseball Challenge (Chapter 6)
Recommended Grade Levels: 2–4

Academic Concepts:
 	
  • **Language Arts.** Reading for understanding, forming relevant questions, persuasive writing, public speaking
     ○ CCSS.ELA-LITERACY.W.3.1. Write opinion pieces on topics or texts, supporting a point of view with reasons.
     ○ CCSS.ELA-LITERACY.RI.3.1. Ask and answer questions to demonstrate understanding of a text, referring explicitly to the text as the basis for the answers.
 	
  • **Math.** Money, addition, subtraction
     ○ CCSS.MATH.CONTENT.3.NBT.A.2. Fluently add and subtract within 1,000, using strategies and algorithms based on place value, properties of operations, and/or the relationship between addition and subtraction.

Essential Question: What items would be a worthwhile use of money when designing a high school baseball facility?
Design Challenge: Design a baseball facility for the high school baseball team using an imaginary $100,000 donation to the program.

Supplies:

- Budget sheet
- iPad with a paint app, green screen app, and teleprompter app

Steps:

- Students read *Roberto Clemente: Pride of the Pittsburgh Pirates* by Jonah Winter in the *Journeys* basal readers to set the background for this project. (This lesson could be transformed into a STEM-infused math lesson on any theme to match other stories instead.)
- Challenge the students to design a baseball facility for the high school baseball team using an imaginary $100,000 donation to the program. (This number could easily be adjusted to reflect the grade and ability level of the students.)
- Give the students a menu of standard and upgrade choices for items to purchase for their facility. (The prices on this sheet were not accurate but made up for the sake of the challenge.) Students were required to budget their $100,000 by prioritizing and selecting items from the list.
- As research, the students interviewed one of our assistant coaches to ask questions about the priorities, safety, comfort, etc. for their baseball facility.
- Then the students used their subtraction and addition skills to budget their materials, spending as much as possible without going over the limit.

Assessment:

- The students designed their facility using a painting app.
- Next, the students used a green screen app to make it look like they were live inside their drawing of the baseball facility and a teleprompter app to type a persuasive essay on why their facility design was best.
- The students defended their facility design by giving a virtual tour of the facility.
- The teacher graded the math on the budget sheet.
- The teacher also assessed the green screen video using a rubric.

Resource G

Moon Rover Lesson Plan

STEM-Infused Lesson Plan Example

Title: Moon Rover Challenge (Chapter 6)
Recommended Grade Levels: K–2

Academic Concepts:
 	
• **Language Arts.** Nonfiction text features
   ○ CCSS.ELA-LITERACY.RI.1.5. Know and use various text features (e.g., headings, tables of contents, glossaries, electronic menus, icons) to locate key facts or information in a text.
 	
• **Science.** Space
   ○ 1-ESS1-1. Use observations of the sun, moon, and stars to describe patterns that can be predicted.

Essential Question: How are human needs different in space?
Design Challenge: Build "arms" for a moon rover that will allow astronauts to collect rocks and other materials from inside the rover.

Supplies:
   • Cardboard tubes   • Paper
   • Straws   • Spoons
   • Masking tape   • Tub of sand
   • Plastic gems or special rocks

Steps:

- Read *Let's Go to the Moon* in the *Journeys* basal or another nonfiction text about moon exploration to build background for the challenge.

- Teacher creates a "moon rover" by cutting a large hole in a trifold display board.

- The students are challenged to build something that will allow them to pick up a moon rock from the tub of sand by sticking it through the hole. (Students' hands cannot go outside of the hole and the rock has to be pulled all the way back in.)

- Students design and improve several times, filling out an Engineering Design Log along the way.

Assessment:

- Students present their "arms" to the class and explain why they help meet needs that are different on the moon.

- Teacher assesses the project using a rubric.

Resource H

Improvement Log

	Draw or photograph your group's project before testing.	What happened when you tested it?	What are you going to change to improve before you test again?	What evidence leads you to believe this will work better?
Test 1				
Test 2				
Test 3				
Test 4				

Resource I

Storm Shelter Lesson Plan

STEM-Infused Lesson Plan Example

Title: Storm Shelter Challenge (Chapter 8)
Recommended Grade Levels: 3–5

Academic Concepts:
 	
 • **Math.** Measurement, money, fractions
     ○ CCSS.MATH.CONTENT.3.NF.A.1. Understand a fraction $1/b$ as the quantity formed by 1 part when a whole is partitioned into b equal parts; understand a fraction a/b as the quantity formed by a parts of size $1/b$.
 	
 • **Science.** Weather, weathering and erosion, how earth changes
     ○ 1-ESS3-1. Make a claim about the merit of a design solution that reduces the impacts of a weather-related hazard.

Essential Question: How does weathering and erosion effect us?
Design Challenge: Build a storm shelter to protect a plastic action figure from the rain and wind BUT you have to build it out of clay made from salt, flour, oil, and water WITHOUT a recipe.
Supplies: • Salt   • Flour   • Oil

(Continued)

(Continued)

- Water
- Large bowls
- Index cards
- Scoop or measuring teaspoon
- Cardboard (to build on)
- Fan (wind simulator)
- Strainer and pitcher of water (rain simulator)

Steps:

- Introduce the challenge to the students. First, tell them they will be building storm shelters, and then add in the challenge of making up their own clay recipe.
- Ask each group to discuss what role each material might play in the dough (i.e., flour for thickening, salt to allow dough to be shaped, water to moisten, oil to smooth).
- Tell each group that they have $20 to spend on materials for their recipe. Each scoop costs $1. (You can actually give students fake money if you have it. You may also want to use Unifix cubes or some other manipulative to represent the money.)
- Have each group write its predicted recipe on its recipe card (index card). This will be the materials students buy initially so remind them not to spend all $20 at first so that they have money left to make improvements.
- Have each group come up to the "store" (a table with materials laid out) and buy their start-up materials from the teacher.
- Students must keep track of their money spent and their recipe throughout the challenge.
- Allow students to mix their materials and then decide what else they need to add in order to improve their clay.
- Students may come up and get additional materials until all of their money is spent.
- When a group has created their dough, they can begin shaping it into a storm shelter.
- When all of the shelters have been built, take the students outside for testing.

- First do a "wind test" by blowing the fan on each shelter.

- Then do a "rain test" by pouring water through the strainer on each shelter.

- Have students determine what fraction of each material their clay was made up of using their recipe cards.

- Based on testing, ask students to vote on which clay resulted in the best shelter.

Assessment:

- In their journals, ask students to write about the following question:
  - How does weathering and erosion shape the earth's surface? Use examples from your project as evidence.

- Grade student journals using a rubric.

Resource J

Lego Lesson Plan

STEM-Infused Lesson Plan Example

Title: Lego Challenge (Chapter 9)
Recommended Grade Levels: K–5
Academic Concepts: • This activity was non-academic—just an introduction to communication and collaboration skills.
Essential Question: What mental pictures do you have in your head? Do you assume other people's mental pictures are the same as yours? How can we build shared understanding?
Design Challenge: Build a model of the word you see on the screen with your partner.
Supplies: • Legos • Pictures (two very different pictures for each word) • File folders (to hide pictures)
Steps: • Push back all of the desks, and pour a trench of Legos down the middle of the classroom floor. • Ask students to sit on both sides of the trench facing a partner across the trench from them.

- Reveal a word on the board. Tell the students they will have to build a model of that object with their partner across the trench using Legos.

- The students on each side of the trench go and look at a picture of that word on their side of the room behind the file folder. (However, the picture on each side is different. For example, for the word TRUCK, one side sees a small pickup while the other sees an 18-wheeler.)

- The students go back to their partner and explain what they saw in the picture before they begin building a model together. (The trick was, at first the students did not know they were looking at two different pictures. They assumed their partner had the same picture in their heads as they had in their own.)

- After they had explained the picture, they built a model that compromised the ideas and input of both students.

Assessment:

- This lesson did not require formal assessment—just a classwide discussion.

Resource K

Tennis Shoe Lesson Plan

STEM-Infused Lesson Plan Example

Title: Sports Technology Tennis Shoe Challenge (Chapter 9)
Recommended Grade Levels: 3–5

Academic Concepts:
 	
• **Language Arts.** Basal reader—*Technology Wins the Game,* compare and contrast
   ○ CCSS.ELA-LITERACY.RI.3.9. Compare and contrast the most important points and key details presented in two texts on the same topic.
 	
• **Science.** Engineering, technology, inventions
   ○ 3-5-ETS1-1. Define a simple design problem reflecting a need or a want that includes specified criteria for success and constraints on materials, time, or cost.

Essential Question: What factors must a sporting equipment designer consider when designing a new technology to enhance a game?
Design Challenge: Design a tennis shoe that your teacher can wear while running.
Supplies: • Cardboard • Fabric • Foam sheets

- Plastic wrap
- Paper
- String (several options)
- Rubber bands
- Tape
- Glue

Steps:

- Read the text *Technology Wins the Game* by Mark Andrews (the *Journeys* third-grade basal).
- Discuss how tennis shoe designs have changed throughout history and the factors that motivated that change.
- Students design a tennis shoe for their teacher to wear as he or she runs down the halls. The design must consider all of the factors that were listed.
- Students fill out the Engineering Design Log throughout the project.
- After students have created their design, they will test their shoe by allowing the teacher to run down the hall in it.
- For each shoe, discuss what factors worked and did not work (comfort, safety, visual appeal, enhancement of the sport, etc.).

Assessment:

- After completing this project and the following one, students wrote a journal comparing and contrasting the priorities of the two designs. (For example, with the tennis shoe, comfort was a very high priority. However, with the helmet, safety was an even higher priority than comfort.)
- Teacher grades journal using a rubric.

Resource L

Helmet Lesson Plan

Title: Sports Technology Helmet Challenge (Chapter 9)

Recommended Grade Levels: 3–5

Academic Concepts:

- **Language Arts.** Basal reader—*Technology Wins the Game*, compare and contrast
  - CCSS.ELA-LITERACY.RI.3.9. Compare and contrast the most important points and key details presented in two texts on the same topic.

- **Science.** Engineering, technology, inventions
  - 3-5-ETS1-1. Define a simple design problem reflecting a need or a want that includes specified criteria for success and constraints on materials, time, or cost.

Essential Question:

What factors must a sporting equipment designer consider when designing a new technology to enhance a game?

Design Challenge:

Design a helmet that will protect your brain (i.e., a water balloon) from getting damaged on impact (i.e., throwing it against a brick wall).

Supplies:

- Cardboard
- Foam sheets
- Paper
- Fabric
- Plastic wrap
- String (several options)

- Rubber bands
- Glue
- Tape

Steps:

- Read the text *Technology Wins the Game* by Mark Andrews (the *Journeys* third-grade basal).
- Discuss how helmet designs have changed throughout history and the factors that motivated that change.
- Students design a helmet for their water balloon. The design must consider all of the factors that were listed.
- Students fill out Engineering Design Log throughout the project.
- After students have created their design, they will test their helmet by throwing it against a brick wall outside.
- For each helmet, discuss what factors worked and did not work (comfort, safety, visual appeal, enhancement of the sport, etc.).

Assessment:

- After completing this project and the previous one, students wrote a journal comparing and contrasting the priorities of the two designs. (For example, with the tennis shoe, comfort was a very high priority. However, with the helmet, safety was an even higher priority than comfort.)
- Teacher grades journal using a rubric.

Resource M

Blank Lesson Plan Template 1

STEM-Infused Lesson Plan

Standards/Objectives:

_____

_____

_____

_____

_____

_____

Connection:

_____

_____

_____

Scenario/Challenge:

_____

_____

_____

_____

_____

_____

_____

EDP	Timeline	Plan
Ask		
Imagine		
Plan		
Create		
Test		
Redesign		
Communicate		

STEM Project Rubric			
Goal	2	1	0
	🙂	😐	☹️
	🙂	😐	☹️
	🙂	😐	☹️
	🙂	😐	☹️
All group members participated respectfully.	🙂	😐	☹️
Total Points:	_____ /10		

Other Assessments or Evidence of Understanding:

_____

_____

_____

_____

_____

_____

_____

_____

Supplies Needed:

_____

_____

_____

_____

_____

Grouping:

_____

_____

_____

_____

_____

Additional Notes:

_____

_____

_____

_____

_____

_____

_____

_____

Resource N

Blank Lesson Plan Template 2

STEM-Infused Lesson Plan Example

Title:
Standards:
Objectives:
Essential Question:
Design Challenge:
Supplies:
Steps:
Assessment:

Resource O

Additional STEM-Infused Activity Ideas

(For more resources related to these lesson ideas, go to www.maryville-schools.org/techpbl and click on K–3 STEM Class Lessons.)

- Students were introduced to magnets and separating mixtures in this challenge. At the beach, you drop your bag just as you are going across the boardwalk. All of your coins and keys spill down into the sand below. Now you must design and build something to retrieve your stuff without getting off the boardwalk. (You don't want to disturb the sand dunes!)

- Students were challenged to design storm shelters that would hold up to wind and water weathering. However, before they could design their shelter, they had to create their own recipe for clay using flour, salt, oil, and warm water. Students also had to budget money to purchase their materials.

- Students designed parachutes to allow plastic frogs to travel to the ground as slowly as possible. They graphed their times each time they tested in Excel.

- First, the students played LightBot to learn how to code a maze. Then, they found "clues" (wooden blocks with a plastic robot glued in certain patterns) around the school. They had to write the code (in LightBot style) for each clue. With each clue, there was a multiple choice of three codes each with a QR code. Scanning each code, the students were told if their answer was correct or not.

- Students redesigned a birdbath to help it freeze more slowly in cold weather. They defended their design by explaining how surface area and insulator versus conductors would affect freezing.

- After learning about the Alaskan Pipeline, students designed and tested a pipeline that could carry oil (actually water) at least 3 yards using giant spools, straws, duct tape, cardboard tubes, and clay.

- After reading *Humpty Dumpty Climbs Again*, a twist on the classic nursery rhyme, students designed an egg catcher to protect Humpty Dumpty if he ever falls off the wall again. Students graphed their data using pictographs.

- Students designed a giant pinball machine using cardboard boxes and cardboard tubes. The goal was to create a track that would allow the tennis ball to roll from the top to the bottom as slowly as possible.

- Students designed and tested environmentally friendly carriers for plastic water bottles.

- Students created Lego robots that matched a prototype. Each table created and improved assembly strategies to make the robots more quickly. They soon found that distribution of labor and assembly lines allowed them to produce more efficiently.

- Students set out boxes on a giant grid according to a diagram. When all boxes were in the right place, they were able to crawl through the box maze. The students then played BotLogic on the iPads to learn basic coding commands. They then wrote the code for our giant box maze.

- Students learned about what can be recycled, composted, or trashed by playing a game called Recycle Roundup on the National Geographic Kids website. Then, they built a "Recycling Machine"—something that would allow them to pick up an object and put it into the recycling bin without touching the object. (They used recycled materials to build!) Once their machine was working, they came up with ways to improve it (such as extending handles so that it could be used without bending down).

- Students researched the needs of a Beanie Baby animal and then built an appropriate habitat for the animal. They took into consideration the food, water, shelter, and space an animal needs in its habitat.

- During their measurement unit, students designed and built paper straw rockets. They tested them and measured the distance they shot up in the air. Then they improved and remeasured.

- Students practiced working with partners and problem-solving as they had to help Fred the Worm put on a life vest and get back on his boat. Fred was a gummy worm, his life vest was a Life Savers candy, his boat was a plastic cup . . . but the catch was that they couldn't use their hands, only paper clips as tools.

- Students did a series of tests on six mystery powders (sugar, salt, flour, corn starch, baking soda, and powdered sugar) to try to figure out what they were. Tests included exploring with the five senses, solubility testing, and testing to see if it reacted with vinegar. Third graders did background research on physical and chemical changes using a Padlet wall.

- In this activity, students learned the important engineering skill of reading and following an instruction manual. Students had to follow instructions in order to put together a 10-piece ink pen. This was challenging for the first graders, but they used perseverance and were eventually able to build a working pen.

- While first graders were learning about animal groups in their classrooms, in STEM, they chose one of the five vertebrate groups (mammals, reptiles, amphibians, fish, and birds) and designed a brand new species that would fit into that group. After planning their design on the iPads, they built a model of the animal using recycled materials. Groups were asked to prove that their animal belonged to a certain group by its distinguishing features.

- Students learned about levers and fulcrums by shooting marshmallows. They tested various materials of different lengths and heights to figure out which allowed them to shoot the farthest.

- Students went on a "Night Hike" with flash lights and looked for nocturnal animals (Beanie Babies) that were camouflaged around the dark room. They were also challenged to design technology to allow humans to adapt to nocturnal activity. They came up with lots of great design ideas such as "Super Pupil Glasses" and "The Super Sniffer!" An additional goal this week was for the students to determine what an A+ technology design would look like. After brainstorming criteria, the students worked with partners to self-assess.

- The challenge was to build a plant that met four requirements: free-standing, between 6 and 10 blocks tall, including four flower parts (petals, leaves, stem, and roots), and all of the colors of the rainbow had to be represented at each table.

- This project was based on Dr. Seuss's *The Lorax*. After reading the story, students were challenged to create a commercial or public service announcement to "speak for the trees." In groups, they wrote skits detailing why we need to protect our trees and ways that kids can help. Next, they recorded their PSAs using an iPad, and the class got to watch it.

- Students used straws and paper clips to build bridges according to an interactive instruction manual in Notability. They then improved the bridge to make it sturdier.

- The students built houses for the three little pigs using any material they chose—Legos, blocks, shoe boxes, construction paper, tape, etc. Then we tested them to see if the "Big Bad Wolf" (aka a hairdryer with googly eyes) could knock it down. Then, they improved and retested. This lesson was an introduction to what engineers do and the engineering design process.

- Students read the story of the Three Billy Goats Gruff in their class. In STEM, they had to design an alternative way for the goats to get from one side of the bridge to the other since the troll was blocking the bridge. Students created catapults, zip lines, etc. for the goats to cross from one giant spool (from telephone wire) to another.

- Third graders designed and built confetti launchers to celebrate the end of state testing. As a class, we created objectives for what a successful launcher should be able to do (i.e., height of launch, distance of launch). Then we brainstormed and planned a design. These amazing launchers were built from recycled material and showed such advanced thinking about scientific concepts such as force, trajectory, and laws of motion. On the day that testing ended, all third graders got to launch confetti in the hallway!

- First, students brainstormed lots of examples of things we have to balance in their lives . . . play and work, healthy food and treats, give and take, spend and save, etc. One third grader even mentioned the commutative property of addition (i.e., 2 + 1 = 1 + 2) as an example of balance! They then were challenged to add objects to the string of a helium balloon to make it hover in the air. They had to work to find just the right balance. We also learned that it is very important for scientists to document each combination that they tried and make small adjustments.

- After learning about natural resources, students were challenged to build dwellings solely out of earth materials: soil, sand, water, straw, sticks, and clay. Then, we tested their dwellings by pouring water on them and blowing a fan on them to see if they could stand up to wind and water weathering!

- Students participated in a webquest called "Catching the Wind." They learned about how windmills work and why they are considered a clean energy source. The next week, they were asked to use what they had learned about wind energy to design and build a sail for a sailboat. They tested their sails by attaching them to a Styrofoam boat on a wire track and a fan. The groups were able to continuously test and improve for 2 weeks.

- Students designed habitats for hermit crabs with consideration for food, water, and shelter. Each class built one habitat, which was connected to all of the other classes' habitats. Each day, we graph which habitat the crabs chose to live in. The students improved their habitats according to the data.

- Students practiced using evidence to formulate a conclusion in this research project. We found out that scientists can't just observe the habits of dinosaurs like they do to find out information about animals that are still living. Instead, they have to look at fossils and find evidence of their habits. Each group selected a dinosaur to study for evidence of its food preference. Students used clues such as teeth, legs, necks, and claws to decide whether their dinosaur was a meat-eater or plant-eater. They also created some pretty crazy dinosaur costumes to wear while presenting to the class.

- Second graders created giant three-dimensional (3-D) structures out of rolled newspapers. They were asked to decompose a model structure into its two-dimensional shapes (hexagons and triangles) and then construct a giant version of the 3-D structure. They also learned to identify the three dimensions of a 3-D shape (length, width, and height) and the parts of a 3-D shape (vertices, edges, and faces).

- Each student worked in a "top secret laboratory" (aka behind a bucket) to build a boat out of aluminum foil. After they built their boats secretly, they were put in groups to help each other improve their boats. They engaged in student-led conversation about what their boats reminded them of, what they were imagining while building the boats, ways they might improve the boats, other examples of things that floated well, etc. Finally, the students took turns floating their boats and asking each other questions such as, "How would you change your boat if you did this project again?" Student-led, respectful, and meaningful conversation was our goal!

- After reading Jerry Pallotta's *Who Would Win?* books, we were inspired to have our own Who Would Win March Madness tournament with first graders in STEM class! The students selected animals that weren't exactly known for their fierceness but were challenged to make them sound tough and dangerous. They read nonfiction books about the animal and chose four facts to put on a playing card for that animal, which they created using an iPad app. Then, the students posted their playing cards on a bracket on a Padlet wall that was displayed at the front of the room. After each group presented their animal and reasons it would win in a fight, the class voted on which animal would win using kahoot.it (which allows students to vote using their iPads and then graphs the results on the screen in the front of the room). The winning animal advanced to the next round where we repeated the process.

- First graders used the scientific method to test which material would be the best insulator—felt, cotton balls, packing peanuts, or cardboard? Each group packet a thermometer into a small plastic bag and sealed it. Then, they put the small bag into a large one. Between the two bags, they stuffed one of the four insulators. After sealing the large bag, they held it under ice water for 5 minutes. They communicated the results of the experiment by making a PowerPoint presentation.

- Students learned that Native Americans used drums for three reasons: celebrations, ceremonies, and war signals. They were then challenged to create a drum that was both loud and nice looking using very few materials: 2 pieces of paper, 10 craft sticks, a handful of beads, a small plastic bowl, a large plastic container, 1 small piece of felt, and 3 cotton balls. The only way to get more materials was to barter with other groups. Then, we used an iPad app to test the volume of our drums. Finally, they improved them to make them louder.

- Students did an inquiry activity in which they were using the scientific method to answer the question: What color is camouflage? The kids formed a hypothesis (many said brown or green) and then did research by reading an informational text. Next, we did our experiment. The kids each took a different colored plastic bug out to the courtyard and found the perfect place to camouflage their insect. After recording their location, they came to the conclusion that camouflage can be any color that allows an animal to blend in to its surroundings. Finally, the students invented their own bug and drew a background for it to camouflage itself.

- After reading about oil spills and their affects on the environment, we simulated an oil spill using a large plastic container, water, and vegetable oil. The students were challenged to create skimmers to clean up the oil spill using cotton balls, netting, felt, pipe cleaners, paper, tape, etc. Students tested their skimmers and then did a digital drawing of what they would do differently if given the chance to improve.

- Students were challenged to design, build, and test an umbrella to keep Smokie the Bear dry during April showers. Students used 1 grocery bag, 1 sheet of paper, 1 sheet of plastic, 10 straws, and 10 craft sticks to solve their challenge. Then we tested the umbrellas with a squirt bottle and teddy bear.

- Students tested the strength of different towers made of Mega Blocks using a homemade wrecking ball. They predicted which tower would be the strongest (single-stacked blocks, double-stacked blocks, or quadruple-stacked blocks) and then counted the number of hits it took to knock various towers down. They used this data to design their own even stronger tower.

Glossary

Assessment   gathering of information and data about a student in order to make instructional decisions and meet the needs of that child

Background knowledge   the concepts, understanding, and assumptions a student already has about a topic before an activity begins; teachers must build background knowledge at the beginning of a lesson in order to create a shared pool of understanding

Common Core State Standards   a set of grade-level standards for English/language arts (ELA) and math written by U.S. national committees and adopted by a number of states

Cross-cutting concepts   concepts or ideas that occur in the curriculum of diverse content areas

Cross-cutting concepts approach (to STEM-infusion)   a STEM-infused lesson that is built beginning with concepts or ideas that occur in the curriculum of diverse content areas

Design challenge   a project in which students design a solution to a real-world problem by applying content knowledge from various content areas

Engineering design process   the process used in a design challenge; the steps are the following: ask, imagine, plan, create, and improve

Essential question   a broad question that helps students focus on the purpose of the lesson or activity; it guides students in bridging the gap between information in different content areas or between content knowledge and real-world application

Fidelity   agreed upon standards of implementation of teaching, defined by educational research and best practices; primarily associated with Response to Intervention (RTI)

Globalization   the increasing interconnectedness of peoples, nations, and economies all over the world as a result of advances in technology

Growth mindset   a term coined by Professor Carol Dweck describing a mindset in which a person believes in an ability to improve; a willingness to use struggles as a learning opportunity

Improvement log   a table in which students record their ideas, results of testing, and plans for improvement multiple times during a design challenge

Productive struggle   stretching students to learn from their effort; accompanied by appropriate support

Relevance   a state in which academic content matters for a student; connected to real-life; applied to real-world situations

Rigor   a state in which academic content is appropriately challenging, as to stretch a student's understanding and encourage growth

Rubrics   a table used to assess various skills or objectives of a project or assignment; also used as a self-reflection tool for students

Scaffolding   providing students with appropriate support so that they are able to succeed in increasingly complicated tasks

Standards-based approach (to STEM-infusion)   a STEM-infused lesson that is built beginning with seemingly unrelated academic standards from diverse content areas

STEM-infusion   using concepts that are part of STEM (such as the engineering design process, creativity, collaboration, problems solving, and technology integration) to teach or practice all subjects

Teacher Individual Exploration Plan (IEP)   a document in which a teacher sets goals for implementing a new initiative; includes goals, an action plan, and a request for additional support or resources; created with an instructional coach or administrator

Thematic approach (to STEM-infusion)   a STEM-infused lesson that is built beginning with a theme from one subject but still pulls in concepts from diverse content areas

21st century skills   communication, collaboration, critical thinking, and creativity; "the 4Cs"

References

Anderson, L. W., & Krathwohl, D. R. (Eds.). (2001). *A taxonomy for learning, teaching and assessing: A revision of Bloom's Taxonomy of educational objectives: Complete edition.* New York, NY: Longman.

Appleberry, J. B. (2000, October 20). *EMU presidential inauguration.* Retrieved November 3, 2014, from http://www.emich.edu/univcomm/releases_archived/appleberry.html

Bruer, J. T. (1999). Neural connections: Some you use, some you lose. *Phi Beta Kappan, 81*(4), 264–277.

Daggett, W. R. (2014). *Rigor/relevance framework: A guide to focusing resources to increase student performance, International Center for Leadership in Education.* Retrieved November 3, 2014, from http://www.leadered.com/pdf/rigor_relevance_frame work_2014.pdf

Dweck, C. S. (2010). *Mindsets and equitable education.* Retrieved January 4, 2015, from http://www.nassp.org/portals/0/content/61209.pdf

Forehand, M. (2005). Bloom's Taxonomy: Original and revised. In M. Orey (Ed.), *Emerging perspectives on learning, teaching, and technology.* Retrieved November 3, 2014, from http://epltt.coe.uga.edu/

National Research Council. (2012). *A framework for K–12 science education: Practices, core ideas, and crosscutting concepts.* Washington, DC: National Academy Press.

Partnership for 21st Century Skills. Retrieved November 1, 2014, from http://www .p21.org

President's Council. (2010). *Prepare and inspire: K-12 education in science, technology, engineering, and math (STEM) for America's future.* Retrieved from https://www .whitehouse.gov/sites/default/files/microsites/ostp/pcast-stem-ed-final.pdf

Schleicher, A. (2010). The case for 21st-century learning. Retrieved November 2, 2014, from http://www.oecd.org/general/thecasefor21st-centurylearning.htm.

Wesson, K. (2011). Education for the real world. Retrieved November 22, 2014, from http://brainworldmagazine.com/education-for-the-real-world/#sthash. 7ERMmMnw.dpuf

Wesson, K. (2012). *The STEM hologram: Several disciplines, one interdependent picture.* Keynote address presented at the NSTA STEM Forum, Atlantic City, NJ.

Wood, D., Bruner, J. S., & Ross, G. (1976). The role of tutoring in problem solving. *Journal of Child Psychology & Psychiatry & Allied Disciplines, 17*(2), 89–100.

Zhao, Y. (2012). *World class learners: Educating creative and entrepreneurial students.* Thousand Oaks, CA: Corwin.

Index

CORWIN

A SAGE Publishing Company

Helping educators make the greatest impact

CORWIN HAS ONE MISSION: to enhance education through intentional professional learning.

We build long-term relationships with our authors, educators, clients, and associations who partner with us to develop and continuously improve the best evidence-based practices that establish and support lifelong learning.